It Happened Just This Way

It Happened Just This Way

M. Apodaca

iUniverse, Inc.
Bloomington

CHAPTER 1
THE BEGINNING

My LIFE BEGAN A LITTLE more than sixty years ago. I went by the name of Betty until I graduated from high school. I always hated that name and would come to find out later that it was not even my legal name. That was not the first of many bitter pills I would have to swallow before coming to that point in my life. I believed I was ready to pack it in, check out, move along to the next level. I wanted to put an end to this meaningless existence. In short, I was ready to see my life end. I was sure I had endured all the suffering one was expected to undergo. Several times in my life, I was sure I was meant to die, but for some unrevealed reason, I obviously never did. Giving birth to my daughter was the greatest joy I ever experienced. Well, not the actual birth—that part was pure hell. But having this remarkable human being in my life was more than I felt I deserved. I had nothing more to accomplish. I had nothing more to look forward to, or so I thought.

To truly understand my despair and the suffering I felt I could no longer bear, let me take you through the ups and downs, the trials and tribulations, and the peaks and valleys that were to become me.

My earliest memory goes back to the age of two. I can remember standing on my bed, gazing out of the window, and pondering the question, "What am I doing with this family?" Even at this young age, I felt I didn't belong. I must have been dropped there by mistake. The monotonous, joyless childhood I was destined for was about to begin. Let me start by painting a picture of the parental unit that brought me into my world of woe.

Back in the 1940s, everybody was getting married. I'm not sure true love was really a requirement—at least it didn't seem to be for my parents. The routine was to get married, have kids, and stay together 'til death do you part. At least they got that part right. The part about love and honor seemed to be just a suggestion, so I don't even mention it. I give them credit for the stamina they had to tolerate each other for almost sixty years.

My dad died of lung cancer at the age of eighty-eight. He was a career army man and apparently not a very good one. In twenty years of service, he never made rank higher than sergeant. Of course, this is not to say he didn't excel at something. In his free time, he was a great consumer of beer. I heard my sister say once that he was a drunk. If that was true, I believe he was a very happy drunk; his mood seemed to improve with each beer. He had a great sense of humor, and everybody loved him—everybody, apparently, except his wife. She had no tolerance for his drinking, but he felt compelled to drink in order to put up with her. This was his second marriage. His first wife had died soon after they were married. That made my mother the second wife, which never sat well with my grandmother. She refused to speak English around us. It was always Spanish. Needless to say, my sisters and I were never pleased to be informed of upcoming visits with her.

My dad gave up drinking shortly after retiring from the army. He became a member of Alcoholics Anonymous and returned to the Catholic Church. By the time of his death, he was a prominent member of the Knights of Columbus. He and my mother apparently patched up their differences, because they actually seemed to enjoy each other's company during those last few years of his life.

My mother was a beautiful young woman, one of twelve children. As a youngster, she worked the land, picking cherries, beets, or whatever was in season. As one of twelve kids at home, she was expected to help with the finances. A couple of my mother's siblings would actually become millionaires. She married my dad at the tender age of nineteen; he was twenty-six. This was pretty much the norm back in the day. But it would have been nice if she had given her choice just a little more thought. To this day she says she doesn't know what made her choose to marry him. Maybe she saw how much everyone else loved him and wanted in on the action. After a short engagement, they married. He had malaria on his wedding day. I can't imagine why he didn't see that as an omen. She was a stay-at-home mom until I was ten years old. At that point, my sisters and I became latchkey kids.

This was the foundation of my childhood. When I wasn't listening to my parents arguing, I was dreaming of having a best friend. I do have two sisters, one older and one younger, but I was never really close to either one. In keeping with my original thought from when I was two, I was truly sure now that I didn't belong to this family. Charlotte, my older sister by two years, was always my dad's favorite. She was a pretty, slender, and smart child who grew into a beautiful woman. Margie, my younger sister by one year, was a little chubby, but also very smart and pretty, and she was my mother's baby. Trouble always seemed to follow her, partly because I used to blame her for things she never actually did. I guess it never occurred to anyone that perhaps she was innocent. Charlotte was always very popular and had more male suitors than she knew what to do with. Even in elementary school, she was getting boxes of candy for Valentine's Day. Margie was only too happy to help her eat them. Me, well . . . the little boys used to call me "Betty Spaghetti" and "Fish Eyes." I guess you can picture what a lovely child I was: small in stature, and always skinny. No boy ever went out of his way for me—not in elementary school, anyway.

CHAPTER 2
The Early Years

W<small>E WERE AN ARMY FAMILY</small> who moved every three years or so. I used this as an excuse for why the little boys teased me. They never had enough time to find my inner beauty—and I was told I had plenty. Isn't that what all homely children are told? I went to kindergarten in Fort Riley, Kansas. I never had a friend, even back then. But I got to ride the school bus with the big kids. I loved the smell of the bus's exhaust and looked forward to it every afternoon, sort of like my treat. It kept me from feeling bad for not having any friends. That might explain why I would have mental problems in years to come.

The only real memory I have of kindergarten is taking naps. At Christmastime, all the kids would try to lay their little mats as close to the Christmas tree as possible. I usually won out, because the others were even more interested in getting a spot by their friends. Since I didn't have any, the teacher made sure I at least had a prize spot on the floor. I should have seen this as a sign of things to come. Oh, well—after school I would get to sniff the fumes again. All was acceptable.

But I was so nervous, the only sin I could come up with was blaming Margie for little indiscretions. So I made up a few. The next week, I had no problem, because now I could confess that I had made up sins the week before. Oh, the drama of being a good Catholic girl.

A short time after my smack to the nose, I had a bad smack to the back of my head. My sisters and I were playing on a merry-go-round. It was my turn to push while they rode; I was pushing from the inside. I did not have very good timing, and I stood up too soon. *Pow!* I was knocked out for sure this time. My sisters dragged me up to our apartment and put me to bed. They wanted to be clear away from me before our mom got home. If I was dead, they could swear that I must have died in my sleep. I had no friends of my own, so I was stuck playing with these little heathens.

I not only longed for a friend, but I also begged my parents for a pet. The answer was always no. They blamed our nomadic ways. I was told it wouldn't be fair to the pet if we had to leave it when we moved. I guess it never occurred to them to take the pet with us. We also never had a yard of our own—another argument against a pet. So I found my own pets. I once had a shoe box I made into a home for my pet snails. I was allowed to keep them as long as they stayed outside, on the balcony. One night, somehow, the lid came off, and by morning, all that remained in my shoe box were bunches of grass and a few slime trails. The mystery still remains today as to how that lid came off. I tried having a goldfish. That seemed pretty easy and not much maintenance. My mother felt bad about the snails, so she cleaned the sink really well with Comet, so the fish could have a nice, clean place to stretch his fins. Turns out the sink still had remnants of the Comet, and my poor fish was dead before I could even give him a name. I made sure he received a proper funeral. The same fate awaited my hamster—not the obvious death by poison, but another funeral just the same. He lasted a little longer than my fish, but the exact cause of death was never determined. I did not have another pet for several years.

Meanwhile, I made it to age nine. At that time, I was sure I was meant to be a nun. I joined a club called the Guardian Angels. I really wanted to join because all the little girls got to wear these cool blue beanies. I also thought I might even find a best friend among these little angels. It didn't happen. But, still feeling I was holy, I built a tiny altar in my bedroom. This lovely little altar had a statue of the Blessed Mother. I scattered several holy cards about, and most important, I placed a candle in the middle. As soon as I lit my candle, *poof!* My altar went up in flame. Of course I blamed Margie. Who would believe sweet Betty, with all of her inner beauty, would do such a thing? Poor thing got her ass beat for playing with fire. It was after this incident that I gave up the idea of becoming a holy nun. Little did I know that the idea would surface again in another ten years?

I still had not given up on the idea of finding a best friend. It was around this time in my life that I kept having a repetitive dream. I was trapped in a maze; night after night, I searched for the door. It never frightened me, and I knew I would never find my way out, but for some reason, I had to keep looking for that door. I thought maybe a friend would be there if I ever found my way out.

My mother had a best friend, Francis. She was a den leader for a Brownie troop. She asked if I would be interested in joining.

Great, I thought—there had to be some available friends there. But no. No best friend could be found, but I did end up growing very close to Francis. When she came over in the mornings to visit with my mother, she would drink my milk for me. My mother was always harping at me about drinking it, but I hated milk. Francis was only too happy to participate in our little covert operation to get rid of it. I always wished she was my mother. She was always laughing and joking, especially with my dad . . . hmm.

During our stay in Germany, my dad bought us a fancy new 1956 Chevy. Francis taught my mother how to drive the stick shift. They would drive down the streets of the little towns, with Mom steering and Francis shifting. They would see how many puddles they could hit so as to splash as many people as they could. They found this game quite amusing. My mother did actually learn to drive a stick. My dad's idea of a pastime was to go for a ride in the country after church. When he came upon an apple orchard, he would stop the car, make us kids be the lookout, and steal as many apples as he could carry before the farmer came running out with his shotgun. We were just a nice Catholic family on a Sunday drive. Did I really belong with these people?

One summer our family went on vacation with Francis's family. We visited castles, had picnic lunches, rented bikes to race around in a beautiful park, and of course attended more carnivals. I was truly happy on that trip. I always made sure I was sitting next to Francis whenever we stopped for meals. She gave me all the attention I had been craving. I felt that her daughter, Cynthia, was the luckiest kid in the world: an only child with parents who could give her anything she wanted. When we were treated to candy, Cynthia got a whole bag to herself, while my sisters and I only got one bag we had to share. In this case I would make sure I sat next to Cynthia. I used to think she could get anything she wanted until I found out what they actually gave her were beatings on a regular basis. I learned rather quickly that the grass is not always greener across the street.

One year, my Uncle Junior, who was a merchant marine, was able to spend Christmas with us. Now, every family has that one uncle or aunt who is admired by all the rest. They have an exciting job, have no partner or kids to tie them down, enjoy one amazing adventure after another, and always seem to have plenty of money. That was Junior, and of course, everyone wanted to be just like him. Every one of his nieces and nephews adored him. Nothing was more exciting than to hear that Uncle Junior was coming over. That would hold true until the dark day of his passing. He only stayed a couple of days that year, but that was truly the best Christmas we had in Germany. The gifts he brought only added to the excitement of his presence. Of all my relatives, I think I look most like him. He was about five foot seven, with big pop eyes, bushy eyebrows, and a loud, contagious laugh. It doesn't sound as if he was handsome, but for some reason, he was. Uncle Junior would remain a constant in my life forever.

Catechism was also a constant in my life while in Germany. Our classes made several field trips to various churches and cathedrals. In those days, the females always had to have their heads covered; field trips were no exception. My mom had three scarves she used for just these occasions. Two of them were silky to the touch, and the third was plaid and scratchy. Guess who always got stuck with the scratchy one. You're right—me.

CHAPTER 4
LEAVING GERMANY

We LEFT GERMANY WHEN I was ten and in the fifth grade. We were told we would be traveling by ship. Only families of four or fewer were permitted to fly. Oh, my God, how exciting! Not only was I about to embark on a new adventure, but I was also sure the kids in the States would be much nicer than the kids in Germany. (I guess I had already forgotten about kindergarten.) *Look out, new best friend—here I come!*

We were due to leave Germany on December 29. My mother told us not to expect a whole lot for Christmas this year, because all of our belongings had already been packed. I thought, *what difference does that make? Santa comes no matter what, right?* Nope. My sister Charlotte was only too happy to inform me that she had knowledge that there was no Santa.

"Don't be an idiot," she said. "Mom and Dad are the ones who get us the gifts." She expected me to believe that the parental unit actually supplied all those great gifts we had been thanking Santa for all these past years. But how could that be? Mom and Dad always seemed so surprised when they saw what

Santa had left. Could I really be the knucklehead Charlotte was telling me I was? Apparently so; my main gift that year was a ball . . . and that was only because it fit nicely into one of the trunks. Of course I was not permitted to bounce the ball in our stateroom; it wore on everyone's nerves. Can't imagine what Santa was thinking when he left me that ball. All I could do with it was roll it back and forth to whichever sister could spare me a few minutes of her time. Regarding that bit of information about Santa, thanks to Charlotte, I had deep sorrows and plunging thoughts for many Christmases to come. A very special part of my heart still believes Charlotte is the knucklehead, not me. There just can't be a world without Santa—not my world, anyway.

The voyage from Germany to New York was the trip from hell. I was so seasick I was sure this time I really would die. Other than being sick and rolling my ball around, the only firm memory I retain of this most disagreeable trip was my dad standing on a chair in front of a porthole, trying to acquire a bit of much-needed fresh air. It seems my mother had been cursed with the dreaded condition we call excess gas. In later years I would come to understand his plight.

I'm not sure how many days we were at sea, but coming upon the sight of the Statue of Liberty still remains one of the most thrilling moments of my sad little life. We arrived not a moment too soon.

My dad's orders were to report to Washington State for his next assignment. That meant a car trip from New York to Washington. Our cool '56 Chevy made the journey with us on the ship. The army gave Dad extended leave, so we were able to spend a few days in Colorado before heading to our new life in the beautiful Northwest. Colorado was the abode of all our relatives, dozens of whom awaited our arrival. God, I hated the thought of relatives. They always felt they had the right to kiss me. For some reason, all my kissing relatives had these soft, mushy, moist lips. Surely I would die before we got to Colorado . . . nope.

Besides my dread of the mushy lips, one other memory stands out of this cross-country venture. Margie got gum stuck in her hair—a real pet peeve of my mother's. I guess this was not a first-time event. Charlotte and I had to get the gum out without the folks suspecting our task. We pulled her hairs out, one by one, around the gum until the entire wad was out. Margie didn't dare make a sound for fear of the consequences. That was the bravest act I have ever witnessed from a nine-year-old. Almost fifty years later, we still laugh about that daunting thirty minutes in the backseat of our cool Chevy on the way to Washington.

Because it was cheaper to buy groceries and have a "picnic" than to eat in restaurants, that is what my dad decided to do. Ring bologna and saltines—what a feast! There may have been a cookie or two thrown in the mix. In those days, you had to buy soda in a six-pack of bottles; no individuals were available. Since there were only five of us, we always had a bottle left over. To keep from fighting over it, we all got to take sips of the soda until the bottle was empty. Of course, we had to sip in turns, so no one got more than another. It didn't matter if we liked the flavor or not—if it was our turn to sip, we sipped.

As my dad did most of the driving, my mom was to read the map for him. That was not really a good idea. She somehow always managed to get us going in the wrong direction. Mom knew my dad would be mad if she told him, so she would usually just wait until he saw a sign showing we were going the wrong way and then plead ignorance. It was easier than being yelled at for incompetence.

Several days later, we arrived in the Denver area. It was nighttime, and the beautiful lights of the city shone like diamonds in the sky from the hills approaching Denver. We knew my grandmother's hot tortillas with lard awaited our arrival. Our mouths were watering. This really was a special treat for us. We were back in the States, and life was good.

We would only stay in Denver a couple of days before heading out for Fort Lewis, Washington. We stayed just long enough to receive the proper amount of kisses. My mother cried again. My grandmother gave my sisters and me each a little box of assorted candies for our trip, which my mother immediately took possession of. She was afraid if we ate them all at once, we would arrive in Washington with no teeth, so the pieces were handed out at appropriate intervals. The balance of the trip was uneventful, no more hair pulling and the crackers were all gone.

CHAPTER 5
Our New Home

W E ARRIVED IN WASHINGTON THE same year the World's Fair was in Seattle. The day we went to the fair just so happened to be the same day Elvis Presley was there filming a new movie. I forgot to mention the fact that we were in Germany the same time he was stationed in Germany. This to me was an omen. I was sure it meant I was destined to be in show business—not necessarily with Elvis, but why else would our paths cross twice in two years? To a lonely ten-year-old, destiny was the only logical explanation. *Oh, my God, I'm going to be a movie star!*

For a while, peace had returned to my naive little heart. It didn't last long. But while we were at the fair, we got our first glimpse of color TV. In Germany, we hadn't watched TV, because it was all in German, which none of us understood. So this new sight got us all excited. That Christmas, we received our best gift ever: a color TV of our own. My poor dad was forever taking the bulbs down to the drugstore to find out which was preventing our beautiful TV from doing the job it was intended. This hunt for a culprit went on for several years.

Thank God for modern technology, as TVs no longer require bulbs.

We were still waiting for housing on base when we rented a little log cabin. This is the first memory I have of wanting to be a cowgirl. I rode an imaginary horse all summer. I circled the house over and over, pretending I was at war with the occupants inside. That didn't take much of a stretch of the imagination. I made pretend campfires and fed my pretend horse Corn Nuts. This was also the first time my sisters actually accused me of being crazy. Why did they think that was the action of a crazy person? A pretend life made it easier to weather the storm that was brewing inside of me. How I longed for a best friend.

That year in school, I actually had a friend for a few weeks. But my mother found out she had worms. I was no longer allowed to enjoy her company. Suffice it to say I was left without one solitary friend. You see, at this stage of my life, I still only possessed that inner beauty. I now also possessed one long, bushy eyebrow across my forehead. To add to my grief, my dad told us we were now moving to the base. I had to leave my precious log cabin and my horse. I didn't think my horse would be happy away from the only home he had ever known. Many tears were shed. But I saw no sense in forcing my poor horse to endure the same fate that awaited me. During this lonely summer, I continued my obsession with the Wild West. My mother told me I must have been a cowgirl in my past life. What past life? Did she mean I had lived before, and for some reason I had to live again? Well, no bones about it. That just validated my first thought: I had been put with this family by mistake. The only way I could see to right this wrong was to die and try again. I was sure my true fate would soon present itself.

While I continued to struggle with my loneliness, I entered the sixth grade. There I met Henry, the sweetest guy I had ever known. He had the curliest brown hair, and of course I thought all our children would look just like him. He never called me names or made fun of my appearance. He actually told his buddies he thought I was cute. Oh, the joy of sixth grade! Everyone knew that we were boyfriend and girlfriend. One day on the playground, the other kids took bets as to whether Henry would give me my first kiss. Unbeknownst to Henry, I was the one who started the bet. But alas, it was not meant to be. Henry would not give me that sweet first kiss. What a sad disappointment to find out he was cuter than he was brave.

I threw myself on a bench and prepared to die. That didn't happen, either. The bell rang, and recess was over.

Sixth grade was also when I found out where babies come from. I had led a very sheltered life, and I had not a clue about the doings of procreation. A girl who was a year older than all the others in my class seemed to have all the answers. And for some reason, she also got special bathroom privileges; she was excused before the rest of us were dismissed. I always wondered why she needed so much privacy. Well, then she told me where the little rascals came from. She also explained something about periods. The very idea of my future fate brought me to the verge of tears. Was all this true? How could women just walk around normally knowing this was expected of them? She said I shouldn't concern myself with all this information yet. After all, I still had never even been kissed. I was very confused and very happy at the same time. I continued in this state until summer.

I thought for sure during one of those glorious summer days that Henry would muster up the courage to do his duty as a boyfriend and give me that damn kiss. But another disappointment was about to befall the "lovely inside" Betty. Henry met Sigred Norsky, a cute little blonde who was already wearing a bra and had normal and separate eyebrows. What chance did I have now? She lived across the street from him, and I was eight blocks away and braless. I did not know what course to pursue. I asked my mother for a bra; I was sure that would solve all my problems. I got the bra, but by that time, Henry was in love with Sigred. If ever there were a reason to die, this surely must be it. But oh no . . . in July of this same summer, I got my first period. I locked myself in the bathroom and cried all day.

Okay, I thought, now this really has to be a reason to die. How can God expect a girl to go forth and blossom with a broken heart and a big pad between her legs? I also got pimples that summer.

Still, somehow, I trudged on. A new girl moved in across the street from us. Her name was Betty Everett. She was my age, but she had been having her period for three months. In my mind, that made her very grown up and worldly. I finally had a best friend. She knew all the latest dances and taught me how to pluck my eyebrows. She threw me down on the bed and straddled my tummy and began to pluck. She told me if I kept them up, she wouldn't have to take this action again. I kept them up.

We hung out for what was left of the summer. My mom wouldn't allow any kids in the house when she was gone, so Betty taught me the latest dance craze, the twist, in our carport. She was very cool. Of course, my sisters never had a good word for her. They were as mean to her as they were to me. One day we were walking down by the lake. Betty fell in. We walked to her house, and she, of course, was soaking wet. When her mother saw her, she proceeded to yell at her for being so dumb as to fall in the lake while she was having her period. I thought, *Oh, my God, is it wrong to get wet while having a period?* For several months after that I was scared to death to take a bath when it was my time of the month. I guess I finally sucked it up, because I continued to bathe. Betty's dad got his orders, and she moved away.

After my friend left, I was swift in finding a new friend. His name was Timmy, a little black fly. I caught him in a jar. I added some nice grass and a little sugar water. Even with all the love and attention I bestowed upon him, he passed sometime during the night. No more pets for me; I couldn't stand the heartbreak of another funeral.

I was once again alone but about to embark on a new journey. I was going to *junior high*. Surely my life would turn around. After all, I had had a boyfriend in sixth grade, so I would probably have two in the seventh grade, and a new best friend.

Look out, world—here I come!

CHAPTER 6
JUNIOR HIGH AND HIGH SCHOOL

O<small>F COURSE</small> C<small>HARLOTTE WAS ALREADY</small> in junior high, and more popular than ever. The other kids on the school bus found out we were sisters. The laughs and snide remarks were not easy to ignore. I mean what the heck? I had plucked my eyebrows now and had a nice new padded bra. *I still have pimples, but give me a break—I'm Charlotte's sister. That should give me some social standing.* Nope. This is when I realized I was the freak of the family, and that realization fell upon my heart with ponderous weight. I was worried and filled with perfect horror at the prospects ahead.

About this time, things changed a little on the home front. Charlotte was still Dad's favorite, but for some reason, I became Mom's favorite. I guess Margie was just too independent to be the baby any longer. She was still getting into plenty of trouble, but she no longer needed my assistance. I think my mom felt really sorry for me. My sisters were pretty and blessed with a clear skin, perfect eyebrows, and perfectly straight teeth. I had none of these. To this day my sisters still feel I am the favorite. Maybe so, but to this day I still envy their clear skin, perfect eyebrows, and straight teeth . . . none of which I have obtained.

I entered junior high with high hopes, but as it turned out, seventh grade was the longest year of my life. I had to be the most homely child ever to walk through those doors—at least that's what my sisters led me to believe. I was sure I wouldn't live through it. The host of woes that awaited me on a daily basis was surely going to prove that I was meant to die a martyr. We'll see—there's still time.

Henry moved away, but wouldn't you know it, Sigrid was in my class. She reminded me almost daily that my first true love had also been my first heartbreak.

I had to take gym class. I was not born to take such a class. I had the hardest time running the track, so I would make sure I got outside before the gym teacher, and I would start at the halfway mark. When I saw her coming, I would start running to make it look as if I were already half done. More than once, she caught me and made me run the track twice. There was no justice in my world. Calisthenics were also bitter pills. How were jumping jacks and squats meant to help a skinny thirteen-year-old girl? We weren't required to take showers that year, thank God, but we were still openly exposed to each other. Oh, how I hated gym class! No one was more uncoordinated or shy than I was.

There was one bright spot in seventh grade: the talent show. I was sure if my sisters and I entered as a singing group, we would win. After all, we all had pretty good voices, and I was still sure I was headed for show biz. But it was not to be. They would rather die than be seen singing with the freak.

So, wading through my sorrows, still with no best friend, I somehow managed to make it to the eighth grade, where I met Manny and Jane. These two people would influence my life, in one way or the other, to this very day.

Jane became the best friend I had been seeking and praying for as long as I could remember. She sat behind me in health class. We did everything together. She was a little on the pudgy side, like the Pillsbury doughboy, which explains why I came to refer to her as "Dough Belly Jane." I think it was just my secret name for her; I didn't address her that way in public. Although a little pudgy, she was very pretty and had a warm and friendly word for everyone she met. I think she's part of the reason I was welcomed into the in crowd . . . or maybe people were finally seeing that inner beauty of mine. Either way, I was finally content with life. Jane was the nicest, kindest person I had ever met. Everyone liked her. Peace gradually returned to my normally sad self. I didn't just have a best friend—I had lots of friends.

I was invited to all the parties of the in crowd. It was at one of these parties where I received my first French kiss. When this boy shoved his tongue in my mouth, I almost had a heart attack. I had never even heard of such an act. I thought he had just made it up. But no—Janie assured me this was a perfectly normal part of making out.

"Don't be silly," she said. "Everybody does it."

Was that really sanitary? And, gross—I didn't know where else that tongue had been. That was almost as horrifying as my first "dirty dance," which happened at the very next party. A little faster than a slow dance, this nasty boy proceeded to wedge his leg in between mine and grind away in perfect rhythm. Continuing in shock and disbelief, I finally broke down and cried. He had awakened an unfamiliar feeling in my loins, and I was most confused. When my friends asked why I was crying, I had to lie. There was no way I could explain what I had just experienced. I couldn't imagine that this was something they would be familiar with. I was beginning to think I was the freak my sisters had labeled me as. I was afraid to even think what the next party would have in store for me.

This year Margie was also in junior high. She had no problem inserting herself into my world. After all, she was Charlotte's sister. Somehow, that fact worked for her. Nobody seemed to care that she was younger than the rest of us. She was pretty and had really big boobs. That gave her the social status she was seeking. We were a small school, about three hundred kids in all. Junior high and high school were combined in the same building, so we all pretty much knew one another. Our house became a regular hangout for all our friends; age didn't matter. Everyone loved our parents, especially my mom. She never minded a few extra bodies around. There were always plenty of sodas and snacks to be had.

Jane's dad—actually her stepdad—transferred to Washington from Oklahoma. She used to tell me about a really cute boy she dated there and how she had been truly devastated to leave. With my words of wisdom on the matter of love—sort of like always being a bridesmaid and never a bride—assured her she would find love again before the semester ended. Oh, curse my wisdom! It would later come to bite me in the ass. Jane, being very cute despite her chubby frame, immediately found a boyfriend. I was quite happy for her, even though all the boys just considered me a really cool friend. We were all still content to hang out together. It didn't really matter if someone had a mate or not. Life was good.

A few months into the semester, a new boy joined our school. He was of about average height compared to all the other eighth-graders, and his wavy black hair and kind brown eyes reflected his Filipino descent. Oh, be still my heart! Could this new jock be my future husband? As it turned out, he had also transferred in from Oklahoma. *Hmmm . . . could this just be a coincidence?* I saw this cutie before Jane. It was love at first sight . . . on my part, anyway. I ran to find my best friend to inform her of my discovery. I excitedly described this new boy and informed her that his name was Manny. I went on and on about this wonderful addition to my life—how cute he was, how he was going to be in two of my classes, and since he was so new he couldn't possibly have a girlfriend yet. You could have knocked me over with a feather.

As it turned out, Manny was the love god Jane had left in Oklahoma. *Okay, God, please take me now. Surely I'm not meant to live through this.* Of all the boys in the world, why did it have to be Manny? I can't believe I didn't die of shock right on the spot. Luckily, I hadn't had time to inform her of my intent to marry him. It seemed he was even more in love with her than she was with him.

Oh, the drama of it all! As fate would have it, I became his best friend. He would spend hours telling me how much her loved Janie and how good it was to see her again. It must have been fate, he thought, that the two of them were back together. We were like the three musketeers; we went everywhere together. My true feelings have not been declared to this very day.

Of course, Jane immediately dumped her current boyfriend to be with Manny. Both were social butterflies: Manny, a jock; and Jane . . . well, all the boys just wanted Jane. The two were constantly breaking up and getting back together. This would go on for the next three years. In every breakup, I was called upon to help weather the storm. Being full of dread, I would always assure each of them that time healed all wounds and that they would soon be back together. Again, I say, damn my words of wisdom! I cannot begin to tell you how many times these two idiots broke up and got back together. They were kind of the joke of the school. Whichever mate either of them chose, that person would know it was only a matter of time before he or she would join the collection of other poor schmucks dumped by these two lovebirds.

During one of these breakups, Manny must have been bored. He offered to give me kissing lessons during our lunch breaks. *Oh, thank you, God, for not taking me yet!* To this day, those lessons remain in the top five most exciting things I remember of my sad little life. Manny would later—about forty years later—meet my daughter and tell her what a good kisser I was in school. What a dope, he didn't even remember that he was the one who had taught me those moves.

One Christmas, Manny and I exchanged gifts. He gave me a bottle of Chanel No. 5. I gave him an ID bracelet (all the rage in the sixties). I was hoping he would someday give it to me to wear, but it was not meant to be. He gave it to Jane. During the next breakup, she gave it back to him—or, I should say, she threw it at him. He, being very gallant, broke it into several pieces to show her he would never give it to another girl. There went three dollars I would never see again. The next year, I gave him a box of hankies. Try tearing those up!

We all spent our summers at the beach. Well, the month of August anyway. June and July were still pretty rainy in Washington. Jane's mother was a very strict woman, and Jane didn't get to go out as often as I did. I report these indulgences with an air of guilt, but sometimes, when Jane wasn't around, I would talk smack about her. What the heck—I had heard all was fair in love and war. It never paid off, though. Manny was smitten with Jane, and that's how it would remain, until our fifteen-year high-school reunion.

It's not to say I never had any boyfriends. A couple of guys found me date worthy. It was better than nothing, so I would pretend to like them back. It seemed like the thing to do. It's not as if they were expecting a lifetime commitment or anything. One of these boys who fell hard for good ol' Betty was Manny's brother, Frank. He was a year younger than me and a little smaller than Manny, but again, nobody seemed to care about age in our little clan. Poor Frankie—he had it bad for me, but my heart belonged to Manny. A blood relative of Manny's wasn't good enough, and it certainly wasn't going to fill the void in my heart. I took him to the sophomore ball when he was only a freshman. Boy, was he all puffed up. But when all I could do was chatter on about my sorrow and lonely heart, Frankie finally threw in the towel. I don't believe he ever told Manny why we broke up. After all, he had his pride, and Manny was always showing him up. No way was he going to let his big brother know that his first girlfriend was pining for another guy. Frankie never knew my true feelings for Manny, but I'm sure he suspected.

During our high-school dances, Manny was always crowned prince and Janie his princess. When I saw the two of them dance, I sometimes felt I could endure it no longer. *Please God, take me now.* And, as if on cue, Manny would come and take me in his arms for a slow dance. He was like an angel coming to me in my loneliness.

Manny was on the football, basketball, and baseball teams. I went to all of his games. Jane only went to the home games. You would think that alone would show him how I felt. But nooo—he just assumed I had school spirit and was there to cheer on all the players. Both of my sisters were cheerleaders. People thought I was there to give support to my family. Could the whole world be that dopey? Didn't they realize by now that I didn't give a damn about them? I actually tried out for cheerleading once. I didn't come close to making it. I tripped myself during the tryouts. The judges felt sorry for me and made a space for me on the drill team. At least I had a uniform, and I pretended that drill team was what I was actually interested in anyway.

High school was beginning to suck. I was the class clown, so to speak. Everybody thought I was so funny, but nobody knew how sad I really was. As long as I had an audience, the world was a lovely place, but when the lights went down and the crowd went home, I had only loneliness for company. I knew my dad was getting ready to retire, and nothing struck terror as deeply in my heart as the idea of leaving Manny and Jane. The days with Manny were the happiest and saddest days of my life, so far.

When my dad retired, I knew we were going to move to Colorado. Oh, no—the dreaded relatives! Worse than that, how could I live without Jane and Manny? Would I ever have another best friend? Could I exist in civilian life? I had been an army brat all my life. What would the new school be like? I did not undertake to answer these questions. I just knew God would not let me live through another heart-wrenching event. I spent most of my last night in Washington with Manny. We made out in the backseat of his older brother's T-Bird. I can't remember where we were parked. I just knew my heart was experiencing the worst pain it had ever known.

Then Manny said those magic words: "If you show me yours, I'll show you mine." Show him what? What did we possibly have that hadn't been shown in the past three years? Oh . . . that. Well, okay. I had never thought about it before, but what the heck—it was Manny. After that night, I was sure I would die if I moved to Colorado. But no—in despair and without hope, I made the car trip from Washington to Colorado. I was a tortured soul. No one could console the devastation of my broken heart.

Civilian life was just as wretched as I had imagined. I missed Manny more than I thought possible. I also missed my period. I wrote him and told him of my concerns. He wrote back with haste. He said no way I could be with child. He had only used his finger, because his penis seemed to have had a mind of its own. He believed his mighty penis didn't want to be the first to deflower me. Oh, okay then—never mind. In later years, I learned what he actually meant was, he couldn't get it up.

CHAPTER 7
COLORADO

CHARLOTTE GRADUATED HIGH SCHOOL THAT spring. She had met a nice soldier when her cheerleading group was asked to cheer for the army's football team. The gentleman (I can't remember his name) was just finishing his tour with the army and was moving back to his home in Texas. He was hoping Charlotte would follow him. And follow she did; the two became engaged. My dad was very upset that she would actually get married in Texas rather than in Washington with her family. As I have shown you, we have never been a close-knit family. I guess it didn't occur to my dad that we could fly to Texas to be a part of the wedding. But it never came to be. It seems the young man had more love for his football than he did for my sister. Heartbroken, Charlotte moved to Denver to stay with my grandmother. She knew we would be moving there in a few months when my dad retired, so the plan was to meet up with us again that fall. I have to admit, I was really looking forward to having her back with us. She found a job as a secretary, but it turns out it was a long commute from my grandma's house.

As fate would have it, Francis, from Germany, lived closer to the job than my grandmother did. Francis welcomed Charlotte with open arms and invited her to move in with her and her family until we arrived in October. That turned out to be a fiasco. Not only had Francis beat her daughter, but she now had a little boy who suffered the same fate. Charlotte was totally disgusted. Luckily she didn't have to endure the situation very long. We seemed to show up in the nick of time. I don't believe Charlotte and Francis ever spoke again.

During those months as a civilian, I was back to having no friends. Margie fared great in Denver. She fit right in and would eventually meet her future husband there. It was during this time that I was forced to get my driver's license. I really didn't want to drive, but for some unknown reason, my mother insisted. It took me three tries, but I was eventually allowed the privilege of taking on the Colorado roadways. I'm sure I passed the test out of sheer pity. The officer told me that if I failed one more time, I would have to try in another county. I felt they were being way too particular, but nobody seemed to care what I thought.

There was nothing memorable about my senior year except the loneness. I didn't get asked to the prom, and I had my picture taken at the wrong studio, so I wasn't even in the yearbook. No trace of Betty could be found in my one and only civilian school. I did have one friend, Peggy, who would be with me later when I became the victim of rape. Peggy was not very attractive, with buck teeth and straight black hair, but she was there for me when I needed a friend.

In a few months, I graduated from high school, but barely. I had to take my birth certificate to school for some reason.

It was at that time I found out that my legal name was not even Betty, the name I had hated all my life. My legal name was actually Marilyn. Turns out when Charlotte was little, she could not pronounce Marilyn, but she could pronounce Betty, my baptismal name. From that day forward, I was Betty. All my school records were under the name of Betty. There was no record that Marilyn had ever attended school. It took a lot of fast talking and a few tears to convince the school board that Betty and Marilyn were one and the same. What kind of mother registers her kid at school under a nickname? Meanwhile, Jane, Manny, and I stayed in close contact via the postal system. Suffice it to say that would have to do me for a while.

As I mentioned, Francis, my mom's best friend from Germany, had also ended up in Denver. She and my mother renewed their old friendship. She evidently renewed her friendship with my dad as well. She once confided in me that he spent the night at her house on a special occasion. I was informed that if I ever told my mom, Francis would skin me alive. I'll bet he did more than just spend the night. Despite this fact, I seemed to be as attached as ever to Francis. Her husband had been diagnosed with multiple sclerosis. This caused him to get medical retirement from the army several years before he had planned. During this time, Francis had another child—a little boy they named Jamie. He was already three years old by the time we reunited. I ended up becoming the babysitter not only for Jamie, but also for his father, who was now almost completely disabled. I helped Francis care for him after school and on weekends. This also gave me school credit for some home-economics class I was taking. Francis exaggerated about how many hours I actually worked for her, and I ended up winning some sort of prize for going above and beyond my duties. We only needed to work ten hours a week, and it appeared I had worked twice that much. Francis said it was only a little white lie, and nobody had gotten hurt. She told me to keep my mouth shut, or it would make her look like a liar. (*Look* like a liar?)

As a graduation present and to thank me for all the babysitting, she took me on a car trip to Mexico with her family. I really don't remember too much of the trip, but I do remember that one night, Francis went out for a "couple of drinks" with two men she met at our motel. Somehow she ended up in jail. They let her out the next morning, and no details would be forthcoming. We were never to speak of this trip again.

Back in Denver, I continued to help with Francis's husband until the day he died. The memory of that day would remain with me for years to come. I was devastated and could not be consoled. It was the first death and funeral I had been exposed to. Meanwhile, Francis's daughter, Cynthia, had joined the army. She was following in her dad's footsteps. Unfortunately she didn't last too long. The army asked her to leave due to the fact that she was taking a bit too much interest in the other ladies in the shower. Oh, my God, really? This was my first introduction to a lesbian. Actually, it seemed she swung both ways; a few months after she got out of the army, she was in a motherly way. This girl seemed really messed up. I guess the guy hadn't just used his finger. I ended up babysitting for her, too.

CHAPTER 8
LIFE AFTER SCHOOL

JANE'S DAD ALSO RETIRED, AND they moved back to Oklahoma. I guess Janie couldn't hack civilian life as effortlessly as I did. She quit school soon after arriving back in Oklahoma. Within a few months, she was married to Jerry, a police officer. I never could understand how she got all those guys, and apparently without much effort. In the following year, she would give birth to her first child, a little girl. They came to visit me in Denver when the baby was about a year old. Our interests were so different at this time that I feared we were losing our friendship.

Manny went on to college and eventually joined the army. Of course, knowing Manny, I didn't figure he would go to Vietnam—not enough women there for him to love. He ended up serving in several branches of the armed forces, always with a higher rank than the one before. He fell in love with a great girl, a nurse. I believe he said she was a marine; I could be wrong. It would turn out that his first child, a girl, would have the same birthday as my daughter. Pretty cool, huh? It would be several years before I saw him again.

Me? I was accepted at Trinidad Junior College. I decided I belonged in law enforcement. My love of the Old West wouldn't surface again for several years. When I found out I would not be able to be the type of cop I had in mind, I gave up the idea of law enforcement. Turns out back then, you had to meet size requirements to become a street cop. I was far from meeting those requirements; I was still the skinny chick from high school. I was told the best I could hope for was to be stuck behind a desk, filing and taking phone calls. Well, no thank you. I greedily longed for new experiences. I wanted some action in my life. I couldn't imagine a life behind a desk. So I decided I would join the Peace Corps. I had to take a really long and involved test. As fate would have it, I scored highest in African vocabulary. It appeared I had nothing to contribute to the Peace Corps. I had no trade—and, apparently, not a very good command of the English language. I was turned down. I was in no hurry to find employment. I suppose I was still trying to find my true calling. What could replace being a cop or a member of the Peace Corps?

Around this time, I decided I would try the army. I could see the world and maybe meet a nice guy to build a life with. Nope. As fate would have it, I got a big "REJECTED" stamped on my paperwork. Seems I was almost ten pounds underweight. You would think they could weigh a girl first, before the written test and way before the medical exam—which, by the way, was a most uncomfortable experience. They have had to have assigned the most brutal doctors in the army to do the pelvic exams. I didn't know it was possible for half a human arm to be inserted into my body while the arm's owner carried on a conversation about the current state of the local football team. Well, it was possible.

Feeling really disheartened about all my latest setbacks, I hung around with Francis's family that summer—the summer of the infamous trip to Mexico. I also spent a lot of time with my cousin Bobby. He would be going off to college in the fall, but we had a great summer on his motorcycle. Bobby was about Manny's size and really fun to be around. He filled my need for a best friend. Besides showing me some action on his bike, he also introduced me to pot. I think we actually had a crush on each other, but being cousins, the best we could do was getting high together. He went off to pursue his artistic talent, and I was once again alone.

I got a part-time job at Target that Christmas. Everyone in my family knew where their Christmas gifts were coming from that year. I only lasted a month at Target. I was let go when they realized I was only charging people for every other item in their carts. I guess I was lucky that I only got fired.

The next summer, I accompanied Charlotte, my older sister, to Arizona. She was going to be married. When we got there, she found out her fella was already married. I had to laugh. I mean, really, who doesn't check this sort of thing out? Was he planning on inviting his current wife to the wedding? What a dope.

A man we had known in Denver just so happened to also be in Arizona. He was only too happy to tend to Charlotte's broken heart and shattered ego. One day, while she was out looking for a job, her friend, Al, introduced me to alcohol—salty dogs, as I recall. After getting me sufficiently drunk, he was preparing to have his way with me. Oops—in walked Charlotte! She was appalled, yelling and screaming at him for what he had done to her poor, naive sister. Thinking I was out cold, they immediately began consoling each other. *Oh, my God! Is that what sex sounds like?* I never did let on that I was wide awake and taking notes. Some years later, he would become her husband number two of five. Charlotte found employment with the airlines and became a stewardess, a job she would hold until she reached retirement (and a job where she also found husbands number three and five).

At the age of nineteen, I was going to dance clubs we called "three-two places." They only sold what was called "three-two beer," a low-alcohol beer, so you only had to be eighteen to gain entrance. On my nineteenth birthday, my girlfriend Peggy took me to one of these clubs to help me celebrate. We both met up with some really cute guys. Mine was a ski instructor in Aspen. When the club closed, we were not quite ready to call it a night. The four of us decided to go for coffee.

My guy was driving and suggested we make a short stop somewhere in a wooded area. Still being naive, I thought that when he asked me to go for a walk, he just wanted to give the two in the back some privacy. It was the first of February and freezing outside, but did that stop him? He led me quite a ways off to a place that had an old car seat under a huge tree. I was raped. He told me I could scream all I wanted—that no one would hear me, not even the two back in the car. He was right. He eventually became annoyed with my screams and stuffed my panties in my mouth. When it was over, he took me back to the car as if nothing had happened. He even offered to give me free ski lessons whenever I was in Aspen.

We were taken back to the club and to our car. I told my friend what had happened. The deed was reported to the police, but nothing was to become of it. Back then it was called date rape, and the fact that I had willingly gotten in the car with this goon meant the authorities had no case to pursue. I went to the hospital and had a rape kit performed. At this time, the police told me that the description I had given them of the rapist was the same one they had received on a couple other occasions. Still no legal action was taken. It was several years before I acknowledged another birthday and a few more before I would go into the woods.

CHAPTER 9
JOINING THE WORKFORCE

LATER THAT YEAR, I FELT it was time to secure permanent employment. My first real job was to deliver car parts for an auto-parts store. On my first day, I was taken to a garage to pick up the truck I would be using to make my deliveries. I was given simple instructions: drive the truck back, get it loaded up, and set out on the first day of my new life. It should have been simple, but I did not know how to drive a stick shift. I couldn't expose my limitations for fear of losing this really cool job. (I should have paid attention in Germany when Francis was instructing my mother.) I asked one of the gentlemen at the garage for a crash course in driving this sort of truck. He was only too happy to oblige. (You see, by now I was no longer the freaky-looking sister of Charlotte and Margie. I was cute! I was still petite, but with an actual girly shape. Short, brown, wavy hair and big, brown eyes finished off the package.) Somehow I got the truck back in one piece, and I now knew how to drive a stick. My boss never did find out why it took me thirty minutes to travel those two miles from the garage to the store. He assumed I was just nervous driving a new vehicle. I thought, *let's just go with that*. My new job was great. I hardly ever had to load or unload the truck. There were always plenty of eager young men to help the cute little gal in a miniskirt. The late sixties were the era of the miniskirts, and I wore them well.

It was at this job I was almost deflowered. On a slow, balmy day, one of my steady customers suggested we "get it on" right there in his garage. Nobody was around, and he said he would be really quick. I knew he really liked me, and the feelings were reciprocal. As fate would have it, his penis had the same mentality as Manny's. Again I walked away being assured that I would not end up in a family way. I met a lot of really nice guys at this job, but none could steal my heart away from Manny.

After a year of delivering my auto parts, I felt it was time to move on to a more grown-up job. After all, I was twenty years old now, and I still felt I was destined for show business. I won a radio contest. It was for a ticket to an old black-and-white film at a new theater about to open to the public. That is where I met the man who would change my life.

Throughout the movie, this man said, he had been watching me and the many expressions I possessed. He asked me if I had ever considered modeling. Would I? I was just happy my looks no longer scared small children. He took a lot of pictures of me at several different locations with several of my "unique expressions." Nothing really came of it. I was never completely comfortable seeing close-ups of my face. The taunting of my sisters would forever be in my memories. This man was involved in all types of show business, mainly making animated commercials. I had been spending a good deal of time with him when I expressed my real passion, which at the time was to become a singer. Barbara Streisand was my idol. I would sing her songs all day long, assuring myself I was beginning to sound more and more like her every day. It just so happened he knew a lady who gave voice lessons. He introduced me to Kit, and I was on my way. *Show business, here I come!*

At this time, my earlier dream of becoming a nun was also being kicked around in my brain. I applied to several convents with no positive results. It was a most confusing time for me. Kit and I hit it off immediately. She agreed to be my vocal coach—for a price, of course.

In order to pay for the singing lessons, I needed a job. I answered a newspaper ad for a reconciler. I had no idea what that was, but it paid more money than I had ever made in the car-parts business. The fat, middle-aged man who interviewed me felt it was okay to run his hand up my leg while we talked. I was still wearing miniskirts; I knew I had the job. It was called a computer center, an up-and-coming business. It employed about twenty-five people: computer operators, keypunch operators, and of course us reconcilers. I would be working nights, so I could pursue my so-called singing career during the day with my lessons.

A few days into the job, I met the owner, Dick. The minute I heard his voice, I was in love. *Oh, dear God, thank you for not taking me during my many earlier requests.* This man smiled at me, and I think I wet myself a little. He was quite a bit older than I was, and—damn!—married. But was it a happy marriage? That was what I kept asking myself, trying to justify our constant flirtations. I was so happy at this job. Knowing Dick was married, I continued to date and flirt with several co-workers—that is, until I found out Dick was firing any guy who went out with me. How was that fair? He could have a whole wife, and I couldn't even have a date.

There was a lady working there—my supervisor, actually—with a nervous habit of running her hands through her hair and chewing on her pencil. She really didn't like the fact the Dick and I got along so well. One night I was running around the office in my stocking feet. She insisted I put my shoes on. I refused, stating that they hurt my feet, and nobody but employees were around anyway. She got so angry she threw a chair across the room, snapped her pencil in half, and yelled at me to get out. She told me I was fired.

I calmly looked at her and just said, "No." That really got her goat. She immediately wrote Dick a long letter and left. When I was sure she had really left, a few of us went upstairs to Dick's office and somehow got the letter opened. She had resigned. Nobody ever mentioned the letter again.

Another night Dick called me into his office. He was naked. Not knowing why, I began to laugh. I was assured this was no laughing matter. Dick assured me we were at the place in our relationship that sex was the next step. Gee, up to this point, he hadn't even bought me a meal. But, okay—he was older, so he must know the rules of a clandestine affair. Are you kidding? Again, I was introduced to a shy penis. Was I ever going to get properly laid? He was quick to point out that this must my fault. He claimed he was unfamiliar with such an outcome. Right. This supposedly unfamiliar outcome would present itself, over the next twenty years, more often than not. I loved this man dearly, but a great lay he was not. I never feared getting pregnant.

I worked for Dick for almost two years. Our friendly encounters were beginning to get in the way of our jobs. One Saturday, I was called into work. Instead of working, I was fired. He said one of us had to go, and since he owned the company, he felt it should be me. Good point. He assured me he would find me another job whenever I was ready. I decided I needed the summer off to pursue my show-business career. Of course, at this same time, I was still trying to get accepted into a convent. Yes, I was a confused young woman.

CHAPTER 10
Moving On

As fate would have it, I heard back from the Carmelite convent, in Oklahoma, of all places. The convent was only a few miles from Jane's house. The nuns had a few concerns. First of all, they said I would need a recommendation from a priest and a former employer, both stating why they felt I had a "calling."

I didn't have a priest, so I had to do some smooth talking to Sister Vangie, a nun in another convent whom I had become friends with. Sister V was small in structure and pretty cute, for a nun. She had baptized my little bird, Harold. I had been afraid he would die and go to bird hell. She did a really professional job, and we all had a little party to celebrate his union with God. Her convent turned me down as an applicant, but I was always welcome as a guest. Sister V knew just the priest I needed to meet to get my recommendation. Get this: his name was Father Dick. He was a tall, slender, balding man—nothing like my Dick. Sister V had known him for several years and was sure he would be able to help me. Turns out they knew each other *very well*. This guy was amazing. He was willing to sign any paper and say anything I asked of him. He was also more than willing to show me everything I would have to give up, should I choose to join the cloister. I did not take him up on his offer at that time, but our day would come. I took lessons from Father Dick and exchanged letters with the good nuns for several months while they got to know me better. They needed to make sure I would be an asset to their little convent.

Meanwhile I was taking voice lessons from Kit. She owned a dance studio and a dance-attire shop and sang with her husband's band. She and the band performed all over Denver. They eventually bought their own nightclub, called Kit's. Between lessons, I would help out in the shop, drive her around, and become sort of a gal Friday. We developed a very close friendship.

Several times I was allowed to sing at the clubs where the band was performing, one being the Playboy Club. When Kit's opened, I took the stage on a weekly basis. I so loved being on stage. The sound of applause was electrifying; there was nothing like it. I truly believed this was my calling. One night, we were singing together. We had a little comedy routine put together.

During one of Kit's solos, a well-liquored customer had the nerve to yell out, "Sit down—we want to hear the little one sing!"

She retorted with, "If you want to hear her sing, buy her a club of her own."

pushed up against the fence on one side and a big climbing tree on the convent side. We agreed I would climb the tree and leave notes for her as to my welfare, and she, in turn, would leave me a cigarette or two—a vice we were both trying to master. Jane knew nothing of nuns or convents and felt sure that once the doors closed behind me, it would mean the end of my existence—thus her request for the notes.

Once inside I was introduced to all the sisters, about twelve in all. Sister Stephen was to take charge of me until I became a postulant. At this time, I was considered an aspirant, the lowest of the low. Sister Stephen was a rather large woman with a face that had a tendency to get red when she was upset. Mother Superior was a little lady who usually had a smile on her face. The other nuns were of various shapes and sizes and always seemed to be busy. I never had a chance to get close to any of them. None were ever considered a friend, although they all seemed to enjoy having me around.

The convent was just as I had imagined: a huge structure made of stone with a tall wall built around the grounds. A tall bell tower was all that could be seen from the street. Sister Stephen showed me to my tiny one-window room, which consisted of a bed, a dresser, a small desk, and of course a chair. I was given my schedule and told of the rules I must follow. The main one was to adhere to their vow of silence. The sisters were only permitted to talk during the recreation hour, which followed dinner. They would be somewhat lenient toward me, assuming I would have several questions about my duties as I came to learn them. I was told not to become bothersome to the other sisters, as many were meditating while tending to their own chores.

So this was how it would be: no meat and no one to talk to. I would be addressed as Sister Marilyn.

My first job was making the white wafers that would be packaged and sent to several parishes to be used in communion. A machine that looked like a giant waffle press was used to make the wafers. They weren't blessed yet, and I was starving, so I didn't think anyone would mind if I ate a few. Actually, I ate quite a few; I shoved them in my mouth by the handful. And everyone did seem to mind.

I was relieved of that chore and told I would now be mowing the lawn. Sister Stephen figured I couldn't get into much trouble outdoors. This was the perfect opportunity to climb the tree and leave Janie a note. I figured she would be pretty concerned by now, seeing as three whole days had passed since I had last seen her. The promised cigarettes were there, and I left a note telling her of my new life behind closed doors before continuing my mowing. I told her of the constant prayers, the meatless meals, the books I was required to read, and my previous job with the wafers.

That night, after last prayers, I went to my room to enjoy my smokes, one after the other. I stuffed a towel under the door, as I'd seen done on TV, to block the smoke from escaping. I thought I was so clever. Life seemed doable at this point. I was a little lonely, but I felt I could endure for God.

The next morning, I found a note slipped under my door asking me to please hand over all forms of tobacco. Seems not only did the sisters become alarmed when smelling smoke, but I had also been spotted the previous day, climbing the tree.

The tree became off-limits before I had a chance to inform Jane.

When Jane did not hear from me for several days, she sent her husband to check on my welfare. I was not aware of the fact, and the good sisters did not bother to share this information with me. Jerry, Jane's husband, was told I was in seclusion and could not have any contact with the outside world at this time. When this conversation was reported back to my friend, she was now sure I was doomed. There was nothing she could do, and she had no way to contact me. She decided to go on about her life and try not to imagine the horrors I must be experiencing. In other words, she tried to forget me. Nice friend.

Meanwhile, the lawn only needed tending to on a weekly basis, so I was given the added task of laundry—washing only, as someone else was in charge of hanging. Picture this: a clothesline full of granny panties and a few pairs of my bikini panties. The nuns were appalled. I was supposed to be wearing the complete aspirant attire, not just the parts they could see. So along with my smokes, I also had to hand over my panties. They issued me a nice new package of big, white granny panties. I was also not allowed to use tampons. There were a few days I felt well diapered, as well as a little hindered in my walk.

During one of my laundry days, the sheets were hung to dry in the warm Oklahoma breeze. One of the sisters happened to be gazing out of her window and noticed little footprints on some of the otherwise clean sheets. Immediately I was blamed for this prank. Why me? Why would I sabotage my own backbreaking task, knowing the burden would fall upon me to not only rewash the sheets, but probably to hang them as well?

"But it wasn't me, Sister Stephen. Why would I do that?"

"Sister Marilyn, you are the only one with such tiny feet," was her reply. "And as to why you would do it, I have no idea."

Try as I might, I could not convince her of my innocence. Somebody was setting me up, and I was on a mission to find the culprit. Nun or no nun, somebody was going down. For punishment, I was told to meditate on a chapter from some holy book I was required to read. After a week, I was still on the first paragraph. I just couldn't get the hang of meditation.

By now I had been at the convent almost two months. I never did identify the nasty little culprit who was trying to interfere with my future as a nun. There were a couple of lesbian nuns whom I felt were responsible. I tried to follow them after recreation, but they kept giving me the slip. Where did these chicks go? Constantly perplexed, I pushed on, but with limited success. I did keep my eye on them, for I felt sure they were guilty.

Because the sisters believed in the vow of silence, they used a giant bell to call everyone to chapel, to meals, to recreation, too just about everything. Each event had its own series of chimes. It was finally my turn to ring for recreation. I knew I had this, and I would show Sister Stephen she could count on me. I rang the bell the number of times necessary to announce recreation.

When I arrived at the rec room, it was empty. That momentary pride was slowly replaced with dread. Where was everyone? I looked up and there stood Sister Stephen, hands on hips, her face a bit redder than usual. Quick as a wink, she grabbed my arm and pulled me out of the room. Seems I had rung the bell to warn of a tornado, not for recreation. The sisters, upon hearing the warning, had gathered all the valuables and run, with treasures in hand, to seek shelter in the far-off basement. When they noticed I was missing, the realization of what had just occurred hit them both as a blessing and a curse—thus the red face and pulling of the arm.

I was eventually forgiven and as sort of a prize for not being disruptive for the past two days, I was given a bicycle. I was told I could ride it anywhere as long as I stayed on the convent grounds and didn't bother the older nuns, who would be in quiet meditation for the rest of the day. Who would have thought that my circling the dorms, singing "The Old Gray Mare" at the top of my lungs, would be annoying? The old nuns reported that the sight of the top of my head going by their windows, over and over, and my singing was not only annoying, but also making them dizzy. The bike was taken away.

I happened to be in the kitchen one day when groceries were being delivered by a kid named Carlos. I'm not sure what acts took place for Carlos to feel he had to teach me to play craps, but that is what was going on when Sister Stephen came in looking for me. Once again I was in the doghouse—actually; I was in the chapel, on my knees, for what seemed to be forever. My help in the kitchen was no longer required. I was truly beginning to have serious doubts about my vocation. I never experienced any bonds of love or sisterly affection, something I noticed being shared among the others.

As I pondered my ability to become a nun, I looked to Mother Superior for advice and counsel. She informed me that although she considered me to be a ray of sunshine for the convent, I also had a very disruptive personality. She did not feel I would be able to adhere to their way of life, and trying to force myself to do so would only break my spirit. I was told to go home for six months, resume the life I had left, and do some serious soul-searching. If, after that time, I felt sure this was the life for me, I could come back. Jane came the next day and rescued me.

Let me just add a note: I did go back six months later. To my dismay, I wasn't even permitted in the front door. Mother said that when she had told me about the six-month retreat, nobody thought I would really come back. She was sorry, but I couldn't come in. The decision had been made for me: I would never be a nun. It's impossible to express the unspeakable displeasure I felt toward the nuns.

I spent a few days with Jane and her family. Somehow, her becoming a wife and mother seemed to have sucked the fun right out of her. She was still my best friend, but a grown-up version of a best friend. We no longer shared the same interests or concerns. She was all about child care and recipes. I was still looking for that memorable lay.

CHAPTER 12
BACK TO CIVILIAN LIFE

I RETURNED HOME FOR SOME MUCH-NEEDED rest, hoping to forget my troubles until a new day would remind me of my sad fate: I was an ex-nun. After serious soul-searching, I came to the same sad conclusion: I really wasn't nun material. I just wished it could have been my decision, not the nuns'.

Would I ever find my niche? Would I ever find the peace of mind Janie seemed to have captured? After another major disappointment, God still seemed to insist that I push on. Oh, well—I still had showbiz.

During my absence, Father Dick left the priesthood. When I was home for good, he tried to reassure me and my shattered heart that I would eventually find my true calling. He also introduced me to that memorable lay I was beginning to wonder even existed. Thank God for His infinite wisdom in not allowing me to leave before experiencing this remarkable feat of man. Although when Father Dick asked me if I wanted to kiss "it," I thought to myself, *Hell, no—I don't know where that thing has been.* He didn't seem to take offense and wasted no time in resuming the task at hand. How could a priest be so knowledgeable of such acts? He claimed to have read a lot of books. Thank God for books! He shared his knowledge with me several times before we parted company for good. It seems Father—or ex-Father—Dick realized he, too, had a different calling. He married a lady with two boys and became a mental-health professional about sixty miles away from me. No use in tempting fate. But thanks to him, I now knew the true joy of sex.

My old boss Dick also awaited my return. He procured that job he had promised me when he fired me those many months ago, at one of his banks. So I was now in the banking business by day and occasionally singing with Kit at night. Some harmony had returned to my still confused and tormented life. I loved Dick so much, I was sure he could see the suffering I endured by his constant absence. If he was that observant, he never let on, and I had my pride—well, some pride. Not enough that I wasn't willing to share him. These few stolen moments would have to satisfy my aching and longing heart.

CHAPTER 13
THERESA AND THE BANK

I APPLIED FOR WORK AT DICK'S bank and met Theresa. She was actually the lady who hired me. She said I had come in looking like someone who needed a home, a bit of a tart with my black tights and silver metallic trench coat. I guess she felt she had to save me.

Theresa would soon become my new best friend and, at times, a mother figure. She was of German descent, along with her husband, Alfred. She was a beautiful woman with short, wavy, frosted hair, a perfect complexion, and an adorable accent. Theresa and Alfred had moved to the States from Tergensee, a small town in Northern Germany, more than twenty years earlier. Without knowing any English when she first arrived, she would work her way up to vice president of the bank that now employed me, fifteen years after she started. Neither she nor Alfred wanted children due to the fact that they had no family in the States to help take care of the offspring should anything happen to either one of them. Me being twenty years their junior sort of filled that gap for them. Theresa was always giving me advice on how to find happiness. Her strongest thought was for me to part ways with Dick. Our situation, she was sure, would only lead to mental suffering on my part. But when it came to Dick, I seemed to have lost any good judgment I at one time may have possessed. The heart wanted what the heart wanted. I think I heard that in a song or something.

I learned many things from my new friend Theresa. She taught me a couple of yummy recipes I still use today, she taught me not to sit on a cold surface for fear of doing damage to my female parts, and she taught me the difference between sexy and crude. These are just a few lessons she instilled in me.

During the six years I worked for Theresa, the date of December 16 kept coming up. I thought it was some German holiday I had forgotten or a special date she had at one time mentioned to me. She kept insisting she had no knowledge of this date. Hmmm. We had lunch together every day at work, and on weekends when her husband was working, I would take her shopping. Theresa never learned to drive. She was always trying to teach me the value of a dollar. Seems I had a hard time hanging onto my money. People were sure I would end up a bag lady. I guess there's still time to prove them right. Every December, I would bring up the sixteenth, and every year she would plead ignorance.

I made many new friends at the bank: Kathleen (Theresa's secretary), Penny Sue Higgins, Bertha Ballbuster, Carol Ann, and Barb, just to mention a few. Bertha was around the same age as Theresa, very tall and skinny and very jealous of the relationship we shared. So, being my immediate supervisor, she did everything she could to keep me away from Theresa—thus the title of Ballbuster.

Kathleen was a newlywed. She was very pretty but a little on the chubby side. She took great pleasure in sharing all the details of her wedding with anyone who would listen. She was more excited about the past events than she was about her new husband. About a year into the marriage, they separated. One night during this separation, Kathleen came up with the brilliant idea of toilet papering her boss's house. She actually had another boss besides Theresa. We borrowed a bunch of toilet paper from a restaurant and proceeded to "decorate" his house. The next day she waited to see if he would mention the mishap. As it turned out, he was late and only too happy to mention the mishap. He made all sorts of threats about what he would do if he ever caught up with the culprits. It was also on this night, during dinner, that Kathleen was laughing while eating a hamburger. At one point, she actually snorted up an onion from her burger. She kept trying to blow it out, but it appeared to be lodged in her sinus cavity. All night she kept trying to snort it out, to no avail. She walked around work for two days blowing her nose, spluttering and smelling that darn onion. It either finally came out or became a permanent part of her brain.

Kathleen and her husband were not getting on too well. They asked me to hold on to their living room furniture to prevent them from having to rent a storage space while they worked out a separation. It was beautiful stuff, so I was happy to oblige. My furniture was crap, so I gave it all away. After a few months of looking for greener pastures, Kathleen decided her husband wasn't so bad after all. A week before Christmas, they came to retrieve their belongings. There I was, sitting in an empty apartment with no one to share my ordeal. Dick was with his wife, and all my other friends were also busy with their mates. What a loser I was.

Carol Ann had been at the bank for about twenty years. She was ten years my senior and had the biggest bug eyes I had ever seen. She always looked surprised. She had remained at her first job right out of high school; she was too shy to apply anywhere else, so she stayed at the bank. We lived next door to each other for about a year and spent a lot of time together on weekends—actually, only the days. This woman had more dates than all the rest of us put together.

One summer, Carol Ann and I planted a garden. It was my idea, and I promised her I would work very hard to keep it up if she would help me. I was all fired up until the weeds started to appear. As it turned out, I was not the kind of woman who was happy to work the land. I gave up on our little masterpiece. Carol Ann took over. She weeded, planted, watered, and eventually harvested a vast array of vegetables. I was impressed. She actually offered to share the harvest, but as it turned out, I didn't even care for vegetables. I don't know what possessed me to start a garden.

Carol Ann had always said she wouldn't get married until she turned forty, and damn if she didn't do it. Right after her fortieth birthday, she met her Mr. Right. We witnessed her proclamation coming true. As far as I know, she stayed married and lived happily ever after.

My friend Barb was a real nutcase. She was also a little chubby, with long, straight blonde hair. She called everyone "Toad." Besides Kathleen, Barb was the only one of us who was married. It was her vast knowledge of lovemaking that kept us laughing. When visiting her home, we were told to overlook any "love juices" that may be splattered about the bedroom. I'm not sure of her exact position at the bank—something to do with the "books." Her boss would later be caught embezzling. I just know she could always pick me up when I was down. She had a great sense of humor. Several years later, her son and my daughter would wind up in the same preschool.

Penny Sue Higgins was the most normal of all of us. She was from Montana and every bit the country girl. I'm not sure of her exact title, either, but she was privy to all the private info and salaries of the bank employees. Try as we may to steal her secrets, she would never let go of a single piece of information. She had a big, shaggy dog named Chipper. Pets were not allowed in most apartments, so she had to keep sneaking him in whenever she moved.

Penny Sue and I once went fishing at Estes Park. Neither one of us knew what we were doing. We found an old, dead worm on the shore and proceeded to use it as bait. As you can imagine, we never caught anything. We had found $100 in the King Soopers parking lot a few months earlier and used that money to finance our fishing trip. Luckily we had enough money left over to buy a nice lunch before we headed home. Eventually Penny Sue found her soul mate and bought a house, and all three of them lived happily ever after—in Florida, I believe.

We all had a good time working at that little bank. Every once in awhile, Dick would show up to meet with Theresa. (This was one of the banks his company reconciled.) I, of course, found every excuse I could think of to be out in the lobby whenever he was scheduled to arrive. One day, while in the lobby, I was trying to get Theresa's attention, so I shot a rubber band. It ended up hitting her smack on the mouth. The look I got from her suggested I need not wait to talk to her or Dick.

When I had been at the bank about four years, Theresa and I ended up in the hospital at the same time. She was diagnosed with breast cancer, me with a benign tumor behind my bladder. We were two floors apart in the hospital, but my friends would come on a daily basis, put me in a wheelchair, and roll me to her floor so I could spend time with my sick friend. We were both out of work about six weeks. Back in the day, people believed in long recoveries. Theresa's prognosis was not favorable. After returning to work, we were even more attached to each other than before. I was determined to take care of her at any cost.

Meanwhile, I gave up my relationship with Kit and singing. I no longer felt the closeness or friendship we had once shared. Kit had once told me that if I didn't like a situation, I should change it, and if I couldn't change it, I should leave it. I wrote her a note with those words of wisdom. I felt my time was better spent with Theresa. But from time to time, a bunch of friends and I would go to a club where Kit was performing. She would always pull me up onstage—I think more to try to embarrass me than to let me sing. A good time was always had by all. This one particular time, Al Pacino and Gene Hackman were in town working on a movie called *Scarecrow*. The exciting part is that Kit had a small part in the film. She invited the two stars to join her at her nightclub and made a big party of the event. I was also there and actually kissed Al Pacino smack on the lips. We were both young and cute in those days. Gene Hackman had fixed his keen eye on Kit, but she, being happily married and a woman of high morals, shut him down.

Theresa continued to fight the cancer that was overtaking her once beautiful and healthy body. For the next year and a half,

I would drive her to several of her doctor appointments and treatments. She underwent another surgery, chemotherapy, and radiation. She eventually had to leave her job. Cancer was winning. I also quit the bank and got a job working nights so I could spend my days taking care of my friend while her husband was at work. Actually, I went back to work for Dick. He promised me he would not fire me again.

My immediate supervisor was a lady named Pluma. We became quite close. Pluma was a heavy smoker with thick red hair. She also had a most wrinkled face—more wrinkled than a woman of forty should have. She knew about the relationship between Dick and myself and was most disturbed by it. As she was always ready to give her opinion about the matter, we had some serious tiffs. She and her husband, Max, became sort of surrogate parents for me. I had had a falling-out with my dad, not really sure why, and had not had a relationship with him for several years. Pluma was handy, always willing to listen to my escapades, and easily shocked with facts about my sex life. The woman had never even heard of oral sex! We would remain friends for the next forty years.

Besides Pluma, a few other interesting characters worked at this company. A lady named Karla, weighing in at about three hundred pounds, could and did eat an entire chicken during our dinner break on more than one occasion. The grease running down her chin was the least disgusting thing about her. I won't go into more vivid details; no one who hasn't met her should have to walk away with the memories.

Another lady had some sort of repulsion to water, or so it seemed. She smelled so bad at times that the boss had to send her home and instruct her not to come back until she had bathed. She also left wet spots on her chair. Hers was the only chair with a person's name on it due to the fact that many of us had mistakenly sat in the chair, unaware of its owner until it was too late.

My favorite personality was Fran. A lady in her fifties, Fran had a smoker's cough and the most wrinkled face I had ever seen—more so than Pluma. She loved to tell stories, with a cigarette in one hand and a bottle of cough syrup in the other, about the days she had been a fan dancer with the CIA. You know, it could have just been true.

Those were a few of the people who distracted me by night so I could be with my friend during the day.

None of the treatments were helping Theresa. Six years after being diagnosed, she was told she had three months left to live. The cancer was now in her liver. I was so devastated by the news; I didn't think I would ever stop crying.

Theresa said, "Don't worry, my little friend. I will not leave you until you are ready." In the time we had left, she wanted me to tell her what I planned to do with my life. She felt that way she would still be a part of it. I told her that someday I planned to move to California and have a baby. I promised I would end things with Dick—something she never quit fretting about.

"You must also promise that if ever you are diagnosed with cancer, you will not let the doctors operate," she said. She was sure this had caused the cancer to spread. I made her that promise and barely left her side.

Two weeks before she died, Teresa slipped into a coma. Dick gave me the time off to be with her. Theresa died on December 16, that dreaded date that had haunted me for several years. She died about an hour after I told her, "It's all right, Theresa. I understand. It's okay if you have to leave now." I was willing to let her go.

While I struggled with my heartrending sorrow, I momentarily took leave of my senses. This time, God *had* to take me. I surely could not go on without Theresa. I loved this woman, and I had never felt so alone and so abandoned in my life. I visited her grave every weekend with fresh flowers. The pain and fear of going on without her were too much to bear. No one could find the words of comfort I so desperately needed—not Dick, or Pluma, or any of my other friends.

A couple of weeks after the funeral, Alfred called and asked me to come over. It seemed Theresa, in her will, had left instructions that I was to receive enough money to make a trip to Germany—a trip the two of us had at one time planned to make together. I would eventually make that trip with my Uncle Junior, the funniest man ever. We would make a stop in Theresa's hometown, where I would meet her younger sister (who would also eventually succumb to breast cancer). On my return from that trip, I would go see Alfred to thank him for making the trip possible. For some reason, he thought I would be willing to show my appreciation in a more carnal way. Was he kidding? Gross—he was Theresa's husband. I never saw him again. He had Theresa dug up and sent her body to Germany. I heard that some years later, he also moved back to Germany, where he, too, lost his life to cancer.

CHAPTER 14
ON TO EUROPE

MY UPCOMING TRIP PROVIDED A distraction from my sadness, and Dick also stepped up to help me grieve. As it turned out, he really did love me. When I went back to work, he allowed me as much time as I needed to mourn. He could fix a lot of things, but this I had to face alone. The grief eventually passed, but not the sadness. I loved this man so much. My weak bladder would still succumb to the sound of his voice. Being around him was the only way I could feel relief from my sorrow.

I had been back with Dick a few months when Uncle Junior and I made our three-week trip to Europe. Armed with my passport, my Eurail pass, and more than enough luggage, we were off on the adventure of a lifetime.

It was May, so I figured the weather would be perfect. We arrived in Frankfurt at 8:00 a.m., exchanged some money, and hopped a train. By nine thirty, we were off to Switzerland, our first stop. We were both suffering from jet lag, so the train ride to Switzerland gave us time to catch a few winks. I was too excited to sleep. Uncle Junior had made this trip several times, so he didn't feel he would miss anything by taking a little snooze. We arrived in Switzerland at about four, had dinner, and were in bed by eight. The little snooze didn't seem to help much. I had bought some postcards at the Frankfurt airport but didn't mail them until arrived at our hotel in Switzerland. Because I had put German stamps on them, I wasn't even sure they would get sent. Having Uncle Junior with me was going to be like having my own personal tour guide.

We spent the entire next day on the train, just taking in the beautiful scenery. It was like riding through a postcard. We met a couple on the train from New Zealand. They thought Uncle Junior and I had delightful accents. The lady and I went window shopping in a little town where we had a forty-five-minute layover. My escort was aware of my ability to spend money, so he usually made sure we stopped for the evening after the stores were closed and left before they opened again in the morning. This was sometimes very annoying. We stopped for the night at Lugano, my uncle's favorite little town in Switzerland. Of course the stores were closed by the time we arrived. It was rainy and cold, but still we walked around and took in the sights. We stopped at an ice-cream vendor. My uncle said if we ate ice cream, we wouldn't notice how cold it was. We would equal out our bodies' temperature. His plan didn't work; I was still freezing, inside and out—and he refused to admit that he had come up with this theory because he was too cheap to get in out of the rain and buy me a meal.

We left for Italy around ten the next morning. It was Sunday, and everything was closed anyway. Uncle Junior somehow hurt his leg during one of our many train changes and limped around for the next couple of days. When we spent some actual time in a particular city, he let me shop my heart out. Meals were also catch-as-catch-can. I do believe the best sandwich I ever had, even to this day, was obtained at the train stations in Germany. The best goulash was had at a train station in Italy.

While in Italy, we spent time in Florence. We arrived on Europe's Labor Day, so naturally, everything was closed. We saw a few churches and paid a visit to a young couple Uncle Junior had stayed with a few years back. Later that afternoon, we went to see the Leaning Tower of Pisa. Now that was impressive. I thought I had climbed to the top only to find out I had only made it to the second level. I was permitted to shop the next day while still in Florence, where we also saw the original David and some Da Vinci works. Whenever we came across a tour group, we would mingle in to catch some free and informative facts. I was taught to be assertive and shameless.

Uncle Junior looked up an old girlfriend from years gone by. We all indulged in a quiet, but scrumptious, lunch at one of those outside cafés I'd seen in the movies. It was good that I enjoyed the food, because I couldn't understand a word of the conversation. It was obvious they were speaking Italian.

Our next stop was Rome. We had a hard time finding a hotel (we never made reservations in advance). When we finally secured one, they only had one room, so we shared. I got the bed; he got the couch, which he somehow managed to fall off of. That next morning, I was informed that I had been moaning in my sleep. I immediately assumed I had engaged in some unplanned orgasms, a condition I am cursed with to this very day. He probably suspected as much, but was too embarrassed to say. We left it at, "Hmmm." We always made sure we had separate rooms from then on.

The weather in Rome was perfect. We saw the Trevi Fountain, the Catacombs, the Parthenon, and, of course, more churches. A funny thing: we ran into the couple we had met earlier, from New Zealand. They just happened to be on the same tour bus going to the Parthenon. I didn't do much shopping in Rome,

only at a few souvenir stands. My uncle kept reminding me of how heavy things could get if I kept making purchases. I think he was more afraid he would have to end up carrying them. Back when we were in Florence, I had bought a pair of blue jeans, but they were way too long. I remembered the girls there wore their jeans rolled up, so I proceed to do the same in Rome. People kept staring at me all day. It seems that the ladies in Rome didn't have the same fashion sense as the ladies in Florence. I made quite a spectacle of myself bumming around the streets of Rome in my rolled-up jeans.

We finally made it to the Vatican—now there's a scene to behold. But one had to be careful. It seems the Vatican used a different currency than the rest of Italy. (Euros had not come to be yet.) They would take Italian money and make change in Vatican money, knowing the whole time we wouldn't be able to spend it outside the Vatican. Italians are very clever characters. I believe Italy was my uncle's second-favorite place.

After the Vatican, we went to the Colosseum. How magnificent! To think actual people, so many years ago, had sat in these very seats, cheering while watching a lion eat some poor schmuck. We came across a gathering of people, and we believed a tour of some sort was in progress. So, as I had been taught,

I mingled right in. Turned out it was a rally for the rights of the Communists. We made haste down the street before the police arrived.

I had never walked so much or seen so many churches in my entire life. My poor feet were killing me. Italy was truly a sight to behold, but what a striking contrast to Switzerland. Everything had been so clean and orderly in Switzerland, and things were just the opposite in Italy. People were driving on the sidewalks, yelling at anyone in their way, and basically making up the laws as they saw fit.

Before leaving Italy, we went to Venice. The day we arrived, it was raining, and the city workers were having a garbage strike. Oh, my God, the stench was almost unbearable, but it was still Venice, and I wanted to shop. But that night, everything was closed, as usual. We secured a room in some far-off hotel before heading for dinner. We dined at Piazza San Marco, one of our finer dining experiences. On the way back to the hotel, we got lost. An old drunk was kind enough to walk us back. The next day, my uncle told me about his money belt. He said if he was so stupid as to trust a total stranger in an intoxicated state again, it would probably be his luck to get knocked over the head and robbed. So I was to make sure the culprit only took his wallet and not his belt. *Yeah, that's what I'll be thinking about!* Was the man mad?

Venice had the best outdoor shopping plaza. I found some really great buys. One of the vendors kissed me right on the lips when I purchased several items without even trying to negotiate. I really liked Venice.

We left Italy for good and headed for Salzburg, Austria. It was cold and rainy all day until we crossed the Austrian border. We shared a compartment on the train with a couple who must have been celebrating something. They were well beyond tipsy, but very entertaining, even without understanding exactly what they were talking about. They knew just enough English to be dangerous. It was bright and sunny when we reached Salzburg, but of course the stores were already closed. So once again, we walked around until we found a nice hotel and restaurant.

The hotel was great. Our rooms were so cute, decorated in perfect Bavarian style. They reminded me of Theresa, and once again the tears were pouring. How I wished I could have made this journey with her.

We didn't hang around Salzburg very long. Uncle Junior was afraid the stores would open.

We left fairly early the next morning and headed back to Germany. Our first stop was Garmisch-Partenkirchen. My family had vacationed here with Francis's family back in my youth. Nothing looked familiar, but I did remember the name. After going to a bank to exchange money, we signed up for a tour of King Ludwig's castle. It was another blast from the past. The weather on the day of our tour was miserable, cold, and rainy. The bus ride took about an hour, and the rain actually stopped when we had to hike six hundred feet straight up the mountain to reach the castle. We saw the most beautiful church on the climb up. I stopped to put in a word with Theresa. The castle itself I did remember from when I had seen it as a child, but it was still magnificent. We got caught in a rainstorm on our way down the hill to our bus. We stopped at the little souvenir shop on the way down. I bought an umbrella; Uncle Jr. bought a plastic pleated rain bonnet like the old ladies wore (it was cheaper than an umbrella and could be stored in a pocket). My God, he looked so ridiculous. Even though we were running, we were laughing so hard we almost missed the bus. My uncle and I were soaked: our shoes, our socks, and even my gloves. When we boarded the bus, Uncle Junior had some white, milky substance running down from his hair onto his face. The ladies on the bus immediately took out hankies and started drying him off. Not one hankie was to be had for me. Wet and freezing, we laughed all the way back to the hotel. His laugh was so infectious that even the people who were annoyed with us had to join in. I never did find out what he had in his hair. It must have been some magic potion that attracted the fräuleins.

When we were crossing from one country to another, we had to get rid of any currency we had for any particular country. When the snack man on the train came around, we loaded up with all sorts of candy and cookies. Turns out I had quite a fondness for sweets. I believe I gained ten pounds during those three weeks, just so I wouldn't end up with money I couldn't spend.

We left for Munich the next morning. I was going to meet Theresa's sister. The weather was lovely, and the stores were open. So before my lunch with Erin, Theresa's sister, I was allowed to shop. And shop I did. After lunch, Erin took Uncle Junior and me back to her house to meet the rest of the family. I was so emotional that I think I cried during most of the visit. I don't believe anyone cared. I could only understand part of the conversations anyway.

The next day, Erin and I took the train to Tergensee, Theresa's hometown. It was just like the pictures I had seen. I had never been there before, but I walked the entire town as if I were coming home. Erin showed me the school Theresa had attended as a child. I remembered the story I had been told about a day when Hitler showed up to address her class. Theresa was overheard making nasty remarks about him to a classmate. She was called to the front of the class, where he proceeded to smack her hands with a wooden ruler. She didn't dare make a fuss of any kind; she wouldn't give him the satisfaction. Her distaste for the Nazis never left her.

I was also shown the house the girls had been born in and their mother's grave. Back in Munich that evening, I went with Erin to her house to bid her family a teary farewell. Tears and sadness aside, it was an unforgettable day.

The next day was, of course, more shopping. Uncle Junior decided we needed to go to Wiesbaden, the little town near the army base where my dad had been stationed so many years ago. That was where I had sustained the injury to my head that I had believed put me in a coma. Unfortunately, nothing at all looked familiar. The weather was sort of crappy, so I didn't do much. We decided to go back to Switzerland, where the weather was more inviting.

We arrived in Geneva to bright sunshine. The stores were closed, of course. We spent a couple of days there before heading back to Frankfurt. Our trip was coming to an end. At the train station, we almost missed our connection. Uncle Junior was following a beautiful girl who he thought was going our way. I think it was just wishful thinking on his part. As it turned out, she was headed in the exact opposite direction.

We had to make an about-face and run like fools to make our train.

It was about a seven-hour ride to Frankfort, but luckily we didn't have any train changes. It was a beautiful commute all the way. Since this would be our last day, Uncle Junior said I could shop all I wanted. Wouldn't you know it was a holiday? All the stores were closed. The zoo was open, so off we went. This was where I first saw how giant birds—I think they were buzzards—shared favors. That is what Uncle Junior called "bird sex." For our last night in Germany, we had a lovely Chinese dinner. I guess we had had our fill of European cuisine. The next morning, we left for the airport.

It was a glorious vacation. I believe that trip was the reason I became so attached to my uncle. I also led myself to believe that Theresa was there with me for the entire trip. I would make this same trip again in a few years, but not with Uncle Junior. That trip would be taken with a co-worker and would be so uneventful I don't feel the need to mention it again. The only good thing about it was that I got back to see my beloved Germany one more time.

CHAPTER 15
ON WITH LIFE

GETTING BACK TO COLORADO, I was both somber and ecstatic. I was sad to leave Germany but very excited to see Dick. We continued our involvement with each other, giving very little thought to the feelings of our family or friends. Did I mention the heart wants what the heart wants? Even though I was thrilled during the times I had with him, I felt a void that Theresa had once filled. I found myself once again without a best friend. I had several gal pals and people I spent time with, but nobody to fill the gap in my heart. I had nobody to share my deepest secrets with, nobody to pick me up when I was down, and nobody to tell that I was pregnant.

As it turned out, I wouldn't have to keep the secret very long. I lost the baby soon after I found out I was with child. It was at this point that Dick and I realized just how intense things had become. Were we willing to bring a child into the picture? We enjoyed going away on long weekends, sneaking out of work for afternoon delights, and of course keeping everyone guessing as to our true relationship. Could I do all those things and still care for a baby? Did I even want a baby? Did he?

By this time, Dick and I had been involved with each other for about ten years. He believes he helped raise me. He certainly did have a most powerful impact in my life. He was my "grown-up Manny." I loved these two men more than anything, but I would never have either one all to myself. I would always be Manny's good buddy and Dick's other woman. There would be company picnics, Christmas parties, and, of course, private meetings in the boss's office. All these things made my heart sing so profoundly that at times I thought it would burst: his beautiful green eyes, his constantly chestnut-brown skin, his keen business sense, and of course that voice. These are a few reasons I would never marry. A few men have had some of these traits, but nobody had the whole package, not even Manny. Of course, as I think about it, neither one of them was a good lay, so I guess sex wasn't a front-runner. To be fair, Manny never had a second chance.

I suppose I'm just not the marrying kind. I have always loved my independence. I'm selfish, I'm argumentative, I'm willful, and a lot of times, I'm ornery. What man wouldn't want that? Actually, I've had a couple marriage proposals. One was from my sister Charlotte's second husband, Al. I turned him down. The following year, he was engaged to her. I guess he just really wanted to be a part of our family. Before they married, he and I went to Las Vegas with another couple. It was strictly a platonic relationship. I wasn't quite twenty-one yet, so I really don't know why we went. That's how memorable the trip was. He was a fun guy, and I didn't see the harm, since no body fluids were ever exchanged. I have a few fond memories of the journey. Our car got a flat tire, which eventually ruined the rim; we had to have money wired to us so we could get home; I met Joe Namath; and I can't forget my first all-you-can-eat buffet for $2.95 (it was 1969).

While I was dating Al—well, I don't really think of it as dating—I was actually dating Dan. You see, I really only hung out with Al. We were like buddies. I don't believe I ever even kissed him. He was a really fun person to be around, and I had known him for several years, so I felt perfectly comfortable with him. He appeared to be no threat whatsoever, even after our little party in Arizona. And after being raped less than two years before, I needed to be around someone I felt safe with. Now, Dan is a whole different story.

This man was in the army and as cheap as they come. He was also about the most beautiful man I had ever seen. He had the most seductive blue eyes and long, black eyelashes; I could only imagine the gorgeous babies we could make. The man was also quite large and had an appetite to match. He would take me to a drive-in movie because they were cheaper than a movie house. That wasn't so bad, but when he went to get us food, he would eat a hamburger and fries while he was waiting in line to pay (a friend told me his secret). Now, I don't know if he didn't want me to know how much he could eat or if he just didn't want to share his food with me. He once drove seventy miles out of his way to get a free lunch. I don't know how many times we frequented new-car lots when free hot dogs were advertised. He would never even test-drive a car. In fact he didn't even own a car; he used mine. We kissed a lot—he was a very sloppy kisser—but never did anything more. About six months into our relationship, he left for Vietnam. By that time, I had a very chafed chin.

Before he left, Dan asked me to think about marriage upon his return. We wrote each other often during that year, but I never acknowledged his proposal. It was during his deployment that he let me know he preferred boys to girls. Was he kidding?

He was gay, and he still wanted to marry me? It seems that since I never pressured him for sex, he figured it wasn't important to me, and I would be content to just be married to a good-looking guy. He also thought we could make beautiful babies, although I don't know how he intended to impregnate me. I was afraid to ask. Dan finished his time in the army and moved to Florida. I never saw him again, but he continued to write me for several years. What a waste!

I wasn't even twenty-one, and I already had two bogus marriage proposals in my repertoire. It was during this time I went to work for Dick's company. I had given up on the idea of marriage. I wanted to be a singer, or a nun, whichever seemed more promising. Somehow, before Dick and I started fooling around, I met a disc jockey from a well-known Denver radio station. Dick didn't actually physically hit on me until I turned twenty-one; he had his principles. I used to take Lynn, the DJ, to Kit's nightclub once in a while. He was in the music business and appreciated my passion for singing. We both worked nights, so dating worked out well for both of us. On occasion I would go along with him and the other radio personalities when they were doing some sort of promotion or other. Free T-shirts and fun times were always available with these guys. After a few months of dating, he surprised me with tickets to see my idol, Barbra Streisand. I was in heaven; she was in Las Vegas. So off I went again to Sin City. But again, there was no sex, just kissing. When we got back, he arranged for me to meet his sister. Apparently he was getting a little more serious than I was. I was just having fun and dreaming about Dick.

Lynn told me he wanted to get a divorce and marry me. Was he kidding? He was married? Not only was he married, but his wife was about to give birth to their first child. *Oh, my God! This really must mean that I am in a coma. Surely things like this don't happen to conscious people.* My relationship with the DJ was officially over. Dick was more than pleased. He never liked the idea of me seeing other men. Yes, even though he was married.

I do believe those were my only official marriage proposals, except for the homeless bum on the street in San Francisco a few years later. I hadn't heard from Manny in a few years. I was busy with the new love of my life, and I heard he was getting married. *Good for him*, I thought. *This way I can concentrate on new business.*

By this time, I was twenty-two, the nuns had sent me packing, Kit had kissed me, Dick had fired me, and my life was now that of a boring bank employee. Sometimes I made up experiences, so my friends would think me not so boring. They all had boyfriends or husbands, and I only had me. Some of the stories were so good I almost believed them myself. If I could remember them, I would share. All I remember is that I kept people entertained. As much as I wanted those adventures, I also enjoyed just being alone. I really did enjoy my own company. I went where I wanted, when I wanted. I never had to make the compromises my friends were always complaining about. I lived and worked where I wanted. I really was quite content with my life—at least I was until my friend Theresa died and I went back to work for Dick.

By this time, I was twenty nine, I had lost a baby, and I was wondering where to go from there. Of course I stayed with Dick; my love for him never wavered. The sound of his voice never failed to make me quiver. The funny thing is, as much as

I loved him, I never wanted to marry him. I suppose I figured if he cheated on his wife, he would no doubt cheat on me as well. She may have put up with the deception, but not me. I vowed to not even think of marriage until I was at least fifty.

I had yet to see a really happy marriage. I wanted my youth to be fun, not washing someone's dirty socks and cooking meal after boring meal. I guess I figured by the time I was fifty, I would be too old to care about such things. Fifty was a lifetime away.

CHAPTER 16
New Decisions

I GOT TIRED OF TRYING TO meet life alone. What I did decide was that I wanted a baby. I wasn't getting any younger, and Dick wasn't getting any better in the sack. It was now or never. I told him of my desire. He asked if I would maybe prefer a house or a new car. A baby, he felt, was just a little too much responsibility. I assured him my wish was only for the baby, not him. That did seem to calm him somewhat. In a few months, I was pregnant, but it was not meant to be. I lost baby number two. I was devastated and downtrodden. I continued in this state for months.

Meanwhile I found a new best friend, Joyce. She was not even five feet tall and had a little Southern accent. Joyce was married and had also decided it was time to start a family. Her husband was more anxious than she was, so we all decided to have a little pot party before trying to get knocked up. We had to make sure all the dope was out of our bodies before we conceived for fear we might give birth to pothead babies. I wanted her to get pregnant first, so she could pave the way for me; I never liked going first for anything. (I hadn't told anyone I had already had two miscarriages.)

The night of our party, we went out driving, looking for some wood for a decoupage project I was working on. We came across a fence in someone's yard that looked as if it were in need of repair. We jumped out of the car and started to rip it up. We were taking what we wanted when all of a sudden, the owner came running out, yelling like a psycho: "What the hell do you think you're doing?" What we were doing was hauling ass as fast as we could.

The decoupage came out really nice. A few months later, Joyce was pregnant.

I told myself if I didn't get pregnant again by the end of the year (1980), I would accept that it was just not meant to be. I would continue to travel life's journey, alone. Then, on December 23, Dick and I met for a little Christmas cheer. We were all snug in bed, and I was sure this would be the best Christmas gift ever. Wrong: he hadn't even gotten all the way inside when he came and went, all within ten seconds. *This really can't be happening.* He had gotten me and the sheets all messed up for no good reason, or so I thought. But somehow, one of his little soldiers made the trip of his life—out of sheer determination, I assumed.

I was pregnant, and I had done it by the end of the year. I knew I must be "in that way" before I even missed my period. My skirts were getting too tight around the waist, and I was craving the strangest things. In February, a week before I turned thirty-two, my doctor made it official: I was with child for the third time. This one had to take. *Dear God*, I prayed, *I know*

I'm a sinner, but I really need this baby. If you protect her in the womb, I'll spend the rest of my life protecting her once she's born. It looked good. The little tyke made it past the three-month mark, something the other two hadn't done.

The hardest part was going to be telling my mother about the baby. I think she still thought I was a virgin. The news would be shocking, I was sure. I waited until after that three-month milestone, just to be sure. I decided to tell her in a public place, so she wouldn't make a big scene. It worked. We were at lunch in Walgreens (they still had food counters back then). Her chin quivered a bit—that was how she started crying—and then she had the nerve to ask me, "Do you know who the father is?" *Is she kidding?* Here I had assumed she thought I was a virgin. Turns out she thought I was a slut. Fine thing!

I assured her, "Yes, I'm quite familiar with the father." Her next response was that she would keep the baby during the week, and I could have it on the weekend. Again, was she kidding? I informed her I was having this baby for me, not for her. She told me not to tell my dad; she would do the deed. Fine with me—I hardly ever spoke to the man anyway. I still don't remember what drove that wedge between us.

That year, 1981, was by far the most amazing year of my life. I was pregnant for most of it. I loved every minute of the pregnancy. Well, okay, maybe not every minute. The first trimester, I was so sick I had to eat while lying down, but I never missed a meal. I was always hungry. I would stop to get something to eat while on the way to meet a friend for lunch. My favorite snack was chili and smoked oysters. And for some reason, I always wanted mashed potatoes for lunch. By this time, Dick and I saw each other almost every day. He gave me money to purchase all the baby things I would need. "I sure hope it's a girl," he kept saying. He loved the ladies no matter what the age. I figured it would be a girl because every time I tried to think of boys' names and said them out loud, the little dickens would give me such a kick, I would yelp. After about the tenth good kick, I switched to girls' names. She was fine with that.

All my old friends from the bank were elated to hear of my condition. My friend Toad had given birth to her second child a few months before I delivered. She had a boy, so she gave me all the pink clothes she had received. I was given a baby shower and eventually moved into my first two-bedroom apartment. I had so much fun decorating the baby's room. I couldn't wait to hold her in my arms.

All my friends were delighted except my old friend Pluma. She didn't like the idea that it was Dick's child. I don't believe we spoke the whole time I was pregnant. She would eventually come around, but I was so happy, I didn't really dwell on it. *I'm going to have a baby!*

I did not know it would hurt so bad to poop during the last month of pregnancy. And I waddled, just like the women on TV. People just don't warn you about these things. *Okay, baby, anytime now.* I almost went into labor in my eighth month when I tried to move a washing machine by myself. It was just a little washer, but too heavy nonetheless. But my sweet baby hung on until the end.

I was not happy during my labor. I had the scariest-looking nurse in the entire hospital. Her hair was pulled back in a tight bun, and she had this giant wart to one side of her nose. If it had been on her nose, I would have sworn she was a witch. Every time I yelled, and it was a lot, she got right in my face and said, "Stop yelling!" Of course I didn't. The pain was so great; I could have sworn the baby was coming out the wrong hole. I was eventually given drugs, which I swore I would never be without again. Some young resident kept coming in to see how far I was dilated. I swear he just came in for kicks, so the last time he stuck his hand inside me, I kicked him in the head. That was the end of the young resident.

My time finally came after six hours of hard labor. The baby should have been born on the eleventh, but the doctor was about to go off shift and asked me not to push for ten more minutes. Was he kidding? Sweet, beautiful Ginny Theresa was born at 12:10 a.m. on September 12. Her eyes were wide open, as if she were asking, "What the hell just happened?"

I have to admit I then did a terrible thing. When the nurse put her naked, messy little body on my chest, I asked, "What am I supposed to do with her?" She was immediately swooped up and carried off. She was brought back to me in a few minutes, all wrapped up, clean and hungry. The crabby nurse showed me how to nurse her. The nurse's mood had been greatly improved by this time. I looked Ginny in the eye and apologized for my stupid outburst. I told her she was my first slimy baby, and I was a little taken aback. I think she understood; to this day, she is always cutting me some slack for my ignorance.

CHAPTER 17
MOTHERHOOD

I WAS ON MATERNITY LEAVE FOR the balance of 1981. Becoming a mother was the most exciting, thrilling, and satisfying event I had ever taken part in. My baby, my daughter, the very best parts of Dick and myself, was no longer just a dream—she was real. I couldn't stop admiring her, touching her tiny, perfect hands, brushing her little wisp of hair, and slathering up her wrinkled little body with baby lotion. I tell her that's why she has such soft skin to this very day.

I got to be a stay-at-home mom for the best three months of my life. I never wanted to take my eyes off of Ginny for fear I would wake up from that dreaded coma I thought I was in. She would have been just a figment of my imagination. There would be no Dick, no Theresa, and worst of all, no baby. But I never woke up, and I enjoyed the only true happiness I had ever known. She was so perfect. I had never known such unconditional love existed. I would just stare at that adorable face. I eventually started calling her Face, her first nickname.

My mother came and stayed with me for two weeks. I don't think the baby ever cried during this time frame. Every time Ginny made the slightest noise, my mother would grab her up from her bassinet and insist the baby was asking for her grandma. She was an excellent grandma. When I had to go back to work, my mother quit her own job so she could babysit. She couldn't stand the thought of a stranger taking care of her granddaughter. My dad was also a big surprise. Although we seldom spoke anymore, he was one of the first people to show up at the hospital after Ginny's birth. He looked at her with such pride. He never really said anything; he just touched my shoulder to show his approval. I don't believe he had ever loved anybody as much as he loved his granddaughter. That would remain true until the day he died.

Ginny was four months old the first time she laughed out loud. I came home from work and walked through the door, and the sight of me caused her to laugh with delight. It also made my milk flow with purpose. I was a mess but so happy to know she shared the love I felt for her. I think every mother is afraid when she goes back to work that her baby will become more attached to the babysitter than to her. Even though we all fear it, I have never known it to happen.

At the tender age of eight months, Ginny accompanied me on my first cruise. We went to Mexico. And of course she was the perfect child. I introduced her to her first fresh banana. While holding it in her little hand, she rolled off the bed in the cabin. Luckily, when she landed on her head, the banana was under it. I was still pretty new at this motherhood stuff and hadn't realized she wouldn't just sit there and eat the darn banana. Luckily, no harm, no foul.

When Ginny was learning to talk, "Mama, Mama" was her first phrase. It was never just one "Mama"—she always had to say it twice, and it usually ended with a question mark. God, how I loved that baby! She was the only baby aboard so she was quite a hit. Did I mention how perfect she was? The people in the cabin next to us didn't even realize there was a baby on board.

Dick sold his company to Citicorp and became a consultant. I was never sure what he consulted on, but it seemed to pay well. He paid me child support until the day he died, although he was never a father to Ginny. When she got older, she referred to him as "The Dick." I'm sure she meant it with the deepest respect.

CHAPTER 18
CALIFORNIA

Gɪɴɴʏ ᴡᴀs ᴇɪɢʜᴛᴇᴇɴ ᴍᴏɴᴛʜs ᴏʟᴅ when she and I moved to California—or maybe I should say "fled to California." My parents loved their one and only grandchild so much—maybe too much—that they were constantly fighting over her. They had reached a really rough spot in their marriage, and the baby seemed to be the only thing that kept them sane. They would fight and argue about every little thing, from the way dinner was cooked to when the lawn got mowed. Meanwhile, their behavior was driving me insane. My sweet baby was turning into a wild brat. Every time I tried to discipline her or simply try to teach her to be respectful, they would interfere and let her do whatever she wanted.

By this time, my sister Charlotte was living in California with husband number three. I had been there once before and really liked California. Charlotte had a good friend who was president of a savings and loan. I met with him for a job interview, at which time there was an earthquake. This should have been a warning to me. I was offered the job and decided I needed to accept it to save my baby from becoming a monster.

I told Dick of my decision and the reason for it. He said I should do whatever I thought was best for me and Ginny. He knew how to find me no matter where I went. He said I could count on him for whatever assistance I needed.

Now I had to tell the folks. They loved this child so much, I knew it would break their hearts to see her go, but I had to do what I felt was best for Ginny. Not only would she be moved away from the only life she had known, but she would also be introduced to her new babysitter—a total stranger. I don't know who took the move harder, me or her.

Luckily, the babysitter was also watching a little boy named Mikey. He was a year older than Ginny, and the two of them became inseparable. Mikey was always holding Ginny's little hand and seemed to give her the comfort she so desperately needed at this devastating time in her young life. I always thanked God for Mikey. I also thanked God for the babysitter, who helped me with the potty-training phase. I had never seen a child more attached to her diapers. She would cry and beg me, in her little two-year-old vocabulary, to please give her back her Pampers. It would break my heart, but she eventually came around and became quite proud of her big-girl panties. She would show anybody who would look.

Charlotte was a big help to me. Not only would she pitch in and babysit, but she knew all the best shopping malls in Northern California. It was at one of these malls where she accidentally tripped Ginny. The poor child fell face-first on the concrete and knocked out her two front teeth. Again, I don't know who took it harder, me or Ginny. My poor baby was only two years old. When people noticed her, they would always ask why her teeth were missing. They surely didn't think she was old enough to have lost them naturally. The story would always immediately bring me to tears. Ginny never seemed to mind. In fact, she was so cute, people used to stop me and comment on what an adorable child she was. And now that she was away from the grandparents, she also had an adorable personality.

Aside from the time spent with the babysitter, my daughter was always around adults. She became more comfortable around adults than with children. I credit those early years for the extraordinary vocabulary she developed.

When she was three, we made our first trip to Disneyland. I don't care what anyone says—three years is too young to take a child on a memorable journey. It costs a boatload of money, and they have absolutely no memory of it at all. It just makes for some really cute pictures. We went again when she was four: still no memories, except this time she informed that we did not need to go back.

Our next adventure was fishing. Now, try to explain to a four-year-old that they have to be very patient while the fish are working up an appetite. Good luck. I opted for the local trout farm. Success! Only thing was, it was so much fun, she wouldn't stop. Now, these people don't care how much fun a kid is having—if you hook that fish, it's yours. And you can't help but hook a fish every single time the line is dropped into the pond. I think we went home with about ten trout that day. My neighbors were quite pleased; my wallet was not. Needless to say, our fishing trips were few and far between.

What we really enjoyed doing was driving to San Francisco. As young as Ginny was, she really enjoyed that city. It would remain one of her favorite places to this very day. It was on the wharf where we indulged in our first taste of frog legs. They were fantastic—tasted almost like chicken. I do suggest that if you have an urge to try them, you really should get them someplace like San Francisco and not Denver. Seems they have a different type of frog, or something.

I left the savings-and-loan bank. The president went to jail for fraud. I had known that earthquake was a bad sign. This is when I started in the electronic-components business. I would remain in this field for the rest of my working career. I answered an ad for a job in inside sales. It sounded easy enough, and I was so ready to get out of banking. The company was privately owned by a couple I would remain friends with for years to come. I was told I was a natural in sales; I had a golden tongue. In a year, I was promoted to outside sales. This included sales trips away from home. Charlotte was still with the airlines, so she was not always available to babysit. My parents were only too happy to hop a plane and take charge for the days I would be gone. By this time, Ginny was three years old and in preschool. The babysitter I had used turned out to be a thief.

The first preschool I put Ginny in was obviously not a good match. One day I went to pick her up and was told not to bring her back. It seemed my little girl had caught the teachers stuffing candy into the mouths of some of the children to quiet them down. Ginny did not hesitate to tell the parents of the children what was happening. She seemed to be concerned about the kids' teeth. So I found another preschool, one closer to my work. This school had some sort of religious affiliation connected to it. Ginny had the habit of saying, "Oh, my God!" whenever she was surprised at something. This did not sit well with the teachers, and I had a devil of a time trying to break her of the habit. At this same time in her life, she kept remembering a past life she had had—her words, not mine. Whenever we got in the car, she would remind me to drive carefully. She would say she had died in a car crash with her last mommy. Can you imagine how that gave me the willies? Needless to say, I always drove with extra care when she was on board.

Life in sunny California was quite pleasant. I continued to work in sales, while Ginny did well in preschool. For some reason, I became very interested in the occult, maybe because Ginny talked about her past life or maybe because there were always psychic fairs going on in the area. Whatever the reason, I was hooked. I of course took my daughter everywhere I went, so she became quite familiar with my new pastime. Books became our passion. Her only wish at the age of four was to be able to read. A few years later, we would go to have our past lives read. She always seemed to die as a child, and I had some major issues with my big mouth. I was told that in my last life, I had been a union worker, and while standing on a soapbox expressing my opinion, I had been shot dead, if you believe that sort of thing.

It was also about this time that my fifteen-year high-school reunion came about. Since our school was so small, it was decided we would have an "all school" reunion. It seemed that everyone who had graduated from 1963 to 1969 was invited. We were all army brats, so many of us had moved away and actually graduated from other schools. We picked the year we did graduate, and that became the class we were part of. And yes, Manny and Dough Belly Jane were back in my life, at least for the weekend. My mother was also invited. The kids all remembered her and wanted her to be there for the Saturday picnic. She was thrilled to be invited and remembered; I was thrilled to have a babysitter. Manny had to bring his wife. She said she didn't trust him to be alone with all his long-lost girlfriends. She was a smart woman. It was at this time that Manny finally fell out of affection for Janie. He thought she looked like a frumpy, middle-aged farmer's wife. (I'm not sure how many farmers' wives he had ever met, but those were his words.) He, of course, looked great—very toned and muscular. I melted in his arms during our one and only slow dance. I believed I still loved Manny.

Someone took a picture of the four of us, me with Ginny and him with his daughter. I still have the picture. I was voted the "most changed." I was no longer the skinny, insecure teenager; I was looking pretty good. Manny's wife never left his side at the dance. She didn't go to the picnic (she was eight months pregnant) but sent her daughter to keep close watch on Daddy. The girl was only six years old, so he couldn't very well ditch her. We all had a fantastic time. It was great seeing all my old schoolmates. We were all in our early thirties, so we still looked pretty good. Some of the boys were being introduced to receding hairlines. I was also the only one there who had had a child out of wedlock. Wow, I got two awards!

One of my sister Charlotte's close friends couldn't make it, as she was in jail. Several girls went to the jail to visit her. What a surprise that was. One of the teachers was also absent. It seems he had gotten a little too friendly with a few too many of his students. He hadn't gone to jail; back in those days, they just lost their jobs.

It was a glorious weekend. That would be the only reunion I would ever attend.

CHAPTER 19
BACK TO COLORADO

CHARLOTTE, WITH HUSBAND NUMBER FOUR, moved to Southern California to sell porn. Neither one of them would be featured in the films. I'm not even sure about the details. The venture didn't pan out anyway. She remained with the airlines and eventually got rid of husband number four. He moved to Las Vegas, and she found husband number five and stayed in Southern California for several years.

That left me without a babysitter, and Ginny was getting ready to start kindergarten. I wasn't really happy in outside sales, and I wasn't sure how I would handle Ginny's after-school needs. I heard the State of California was hiring meter maids. How perfect would that be? I could ride around in those little three-wheeled cars all day and watch people cry when I gave them a ticket. I could be off the same days Ginny was off—at least I assumed the schools and state offices were closed at the same time. One evening I went to take the test all government employees are required to take. I figured I would ace the test; after all, I had an IQ of 132. How much trouble could it be? It was not meant to be; I flunked the test with flying colors. The main question that kept coming back to me was, "How many states are there?" Fifty-two, right? And if you think that, don't ever insist that you are right. It seems state board examiners don't have much of a sense of humor. How could someone so smart be so dumb?

Against my better judgment, but out of sheer need, I decided to move back to Colorado. I had sent Ginny to her grandparents for a couple of weeks, so the timing worked out perfectly. While she was gone, I did all the packing and arranged for the movers to get our belongings back to Denver. My dad was so happy we were coming home that he footed the entire bill. My sister Margie helped me drive my car back. I had found an apartment a few miles from my parents' house, and they were thrilled at the prospect of helping with the babysitting. I was less than thrilled, but I felt I had no choice, at least for the time being. My baby was going into kindergarten.

Now the excitement would begin. It was not quite time for school to start, so I had to enroll Ginny in another preschool. I did not want her spending all her time with the grandparents and undoing all the good that had come from our time in California. She was very unhappy at the first school I put her in. She would wake up every morning begging me not to send her back. Now, not even a naive parent could ignore those pleas. Obviously something was wrong. I confronted the school's director. She assured me that Ginny was just suffering from separation anxiety, and I needed to give her more time to adjust. I didn't buy it.

So off I went, looking for another preschool—number four. We didn't fare much better; she cried from the minute I dropped her off until I picked her up. I snuck a peek one day to see how she was doing. There stood my baby, bag of Cheerios in hand, standing all by herself and crying. No one was even trying to comfort her. I stormed in, grabbed Ginny, and marched out, not even giving them the satisfaction of an explanation.

I gave preschool one more try. Surely number five would be the perfect place for her. This school turned out to be the same one my old friend The Toad sent her son to. I wasn't aware of that fact until one day I was picking Ginny up and she informed me that a mean boy had punched her in the stomach. Being the protective mother bear, I asked her to point out the little delinquent. Wouldn't you know? It turned out to be my friend's little boy. The Toad and I had a good laugh, but I informed her that if her kid hit mine again, I would punch her in the stomach. The laughing stopped.

It was a successful few months. Their class was chosen to be in a commercial advertising the school for the upcoming fall enrollment. I was very excited for Ginny. She was very annoyed. It turned out not all the kids took direction as well as mine. She told the lady in charge that if they had to do one more take, she was out. She couldn't understand why some kids had such a hard time running when instructed to run. It looked like showbiz was not in Ginny's future. She finally graduated from preschool, and I was sure all my troubles were over.

I secured a job working for an electronics distributor. This would be an inside sales position, which made me very happy. I now realized I needed a telephone between me and the customer to be most effective. It seemed my golden tongue got a little tied up when I was face-to-face with a stranger, especially when I felt they knew more about the product than I did. I was quite successful at this job and met some really nice people who would remain in my life for several years to come. My favorite was Gerald. He could always make me laugh with the crazy stories of his day-to-day life. His mother was quite the character and gave him a run for his money. He called her on a daily basis just to annoy her. For some reason, which I don't recall, Gerald did not drive. He was always smooth-talking one of his fellow co-workers for rides everywhere he needed to go. A couple of us even took him to a jewelry store to buy an engagement ring during one of our lunch breaks.

Another good friend was Pauline. Now this woman really had a golden tongue. She could sell anybody anything. She was always winning prizes for the amount of product she sold. She claimed to have furnished almost her entire townhouse with her winnings. I believe she did. One day Gerald bragged to us about the fact that he could take a shower in three minutes. Of course we didn't believe him, so during another lunch, we made him prove it. We drove to his apartment and set the timer. Well, it appears he could do it. I even smelled various parts of his body to make sure he had used soap. Pauline and I proceeded to eat our lunches, which we had brought along in the assumption that we would have lots of time to eat while he showered.

Gerald would eventually become district manager of a well-known cable company. He did very well for himself while never losing his great sense of humor. His was one of only four weddings I have ever attended. I never believed in marriage and refused to take part in them. My attendance of his wedding shows how much I cared for him. We still manage to talk to each other at least on a yearly basis. My daughter was five years old when she first met Gerald. She still asks about him when she meets a portly fellow with a sense of humor.

I have to admit that during my time at this job, I developed a major crush on a silver-tongued telephone voice. Every time he called, my heart would skip a beat or two. He admitted to feeling the same passion, so of course we had to meet. He came to the office to pick up a few things he had ordered instead of using the usual delivery system. Oh, my God! He was about five-six and sported a bushy mustache which was trying to hide the most crooked front teeth I had ever seen. I won't even acknowledge his haircut. But that voice . . . oh, my God! Well, who was I to be so discriminating? I had the next day off, Ginny had school, and I have no idea what he told his office about his absence. We spent the entire day doing things I had never even known were legal. His sexual experience was every bit equal to his magnificent voice. Needless to say, I was walking very poorly the next day.

We had several rendezvous of this sort before he confided in me that he was married. Was he kidding? How could he seem like such a nice guy and be such a schmuck? Oh, well—easy come, easy go. I was sure I was not meant to have a guy of my own. Dick, meanwhile, was always ready to step in.

I attended my first PTA meeting in the fall of 1986, the same year I met Gerald and Pauline. I was by far the oldest mother there. I had had my baby at the ripe old age of 32, so I was now 37. These ladies all looked to be in their twenties. I was one of the first people to show up. I sat in the third row about four chairs in. When the rest started to arrive, they sat everywhere except next to me. I wondered what that was all about. Why wouldn't anybody sit next to me? I felt really embarrassed and self-conscious. This would only be the beginning of my awkward experiences involving Ginny's schooling.

I volunteered to be on a committee with the PTA, thinking this would make me feel more accepted. I lasted one month. I seemed to be the only working mother, and the assignment I was given involved me making a lot of phone calls during the day. I had to work, so that did not suit me. Instead of assigning me a new task, I was told my services would not be needed. Fine by me! I don't believe I ever attended another PTA meeting.

Kindergarten was not staring out on the right foot. During the Christmas break, Ginny told her teacher that if she didn't start teaching her something, she wasn't coming back. It seems she had learned the same material in preschool and wanted to move on to a more challenging curriculum. It was at this point I found out that my daughter was borderline genius. She was bored to death throughout her elementary years but would not allow herself to be put in advanced classes; she wanted to remain with her friends. Ginny finally learned to read, and I couldn't keep her out of the bookstores. She read everything and developed a vast vocabulary that shocked most of her teachers. She was usually talking like the characters in her books and not at all like the children in her classes. This sometimes caused her to feel like an outcast. The two of us seemed to exist in our own little world.

During these years, Ginny became very close to her grandpa. He took her everywhere. She turned into a little bowling prodigy. By the time she was eight, her average was well over 250. She swam like a fish and could hit a softball out of the field, all before the age of eleven. She learned all of these skills from my dad. There was nothing he wouldn't do for her. When she was eight, he took her to open her first savings account. She made deposits on a weekly basis from her allowance and money her grandparents gave her. The tellers at the bank grew quite fond of her and looked forward to the two of them coming in to attend to their banking business. That money management has stuck with her to this very day. She will never allow herself to be dependent on anyone, including the social security office.

I worked for the distributor, with Gerald and Pauline, for almost three years. Dick and I remained as we always had been, sneaking time away together as the cosmos would have it. We did manage a couple of trips to New York City, a weekend in Houston now and then, several trips to San Francisco, and of course time at his condo in the mountains. All was stolen time, and I felt very guilty leaving my daughter. She never seemed to mind, because in those early years, she loved staying with her grandparents. My mom let her have my old bedroom as her own. Ginny insisted on paying rent ($2 a month) to ensure her own privacy. Of course there was also the colorful sign on the door warning against any uninvited entry.

At age nine, with the money from her savings, Ginny decided it was time for us to get a little dog. We had already tried a cat, a mouse, and various birds. She really felt she was ready for her own dog. We answered an ad in the paper for some Malteses that were ready to leave their mother. There were four or five to choose from. She decided on a male we named Scruffy. When we got home with the new member of our family, Ginny confided in me that she had originally chosen another puppy, but she had accidentally dropped him on his head and was afraid he may have suffered brain damage. That is how she had come to pick Scruffy.

Love was in our house, along with an untrained puppy who cried all night. We were living in a rented townhouse at the time. Somehow the puppy got out when we were leaving for school. He got hit by a car and almost died. A teenager walking home from school saw the accident, took little Scruffy to a vet, and left word at the animal shelter in case anyone called looking for him. To this day, I thank God for that young man. I never did learn his identity, but Scruffy received the attention he needed, and we caught up with him that evening. He had several broken ribs, and a nurse had actually breathed life back into his little body.

Several days and several thousand dollars later, we had Scruffy back home. His entire body was one big bandage. It didn't seem to bother him, but Ginny pushed him around in her baby stroller, just to be sure. She fed him water from her old baby bottle and loved this little guy like you wouldn't believe. About this time, the lady who owned the townhouse decided she wanted it back, so we had to move. Our new apartment was only a few miles away, but they did not allow animals. Scruffy was taken to the grandparents' house to live. My dad was thrilled to death . . . my mom, not so much. She never really cared for animals, but she could not say no to Ginny. It seemed Ginny spent about as much time with the grandparents as she did with me, so little Scruffy never really had time to miss her. He had a big yard and an older dog, Max, to play with. Max also helped with the potty training of young Scruffy. When Ginny's grandpa went on daily five-mile walks, he now went with two dogs in tow. Life seemed good for everyone.

CHAPTER 20
MOVING FORWARD

Dᴜʀɪɴɢ ᴛʜɪꜱ ᴛɪᴍᴇ, I ʟᴇꜰᴛ the distributor and went to work for a manufacturer's rep. It was a small company owned by two gentlemen. This was the same sort of company I had worked for in California when I first entered this particular field. Chuck and John were the owners. Gale and Bill were the outside sales people. These names will mean something as we move along a few years.

Chuck was in the process of getting a divorce when I was first hired. Gale was married, but not happily. See where this is going? John was happily married, and Bill was about to get married. I was working inside sales along with two other ladies. Gale and I hit it off right away; I think that's because none of the other ladies liked her, and I was happy to be her right-hand man, so to speak. If people thought she was hard to deal with in the beginning, they hadn't seen anything yet. I had worked for this company a couple of months when Chuck and Gale made the announcement that they were dating. Somehow they had both secured their divorces from their mates just in the nick of time (I'm sure). Nobody was overjoyed with the news, but life went on. A year into the relationship, they announced they were now getting married. Now people were really unhappy.

The ladies in the office decided to give Gale a bridal shower of sorts. We took her out drinking, mostly just to mess with her. We needed the booze to spend all that time with her. She did confide one little delicacy: it seems that Chuck's manhood was the same size and shape of the neck of the beer bottle she was sucking on. I guess she felt we needed to know that.

At work, Gale became a complete control freak. She had to know where every penny was going—every purchase from office products to the gas the outside salespeople were using. Nothing was off limits. She had a meeting with the inside-sales ladies. She wanted to make sure we weren't using too much toilet paper and especially that we weren't flushing our lady products down her precious toilets (Chuck owned the building).

Chuck and Gale went to Hawaii on their honeymoon, and laughter came back to the office for two whole weeks. Of course they called in every day, just to make sure we were all working. They said it was to see if we needed them. I guess it didn't matter that John, Chuck's partner, was still there. But that wouldn't last for long. A few months after the marriage, John sold his share of the company to Chuck. He just couldn't deal with Gale having so much control. John's leaving was a sad day for us all. I had grown quite fond of him, and things would never be the same at that little company again.

For some reason, Ginny had grown attached to Gale. I think she was fascinated by her makeup style. (You would have to see it to believe it.) Gale and I maintained our friendship for several years. It would come to an abrupt end one day after we went to a movie she kept harping about. I sternly told her to "get over it." Those three words ended a friendship that spanned over fifteen years. Who knew she was that sensitive? She walked away from me, and we never spoke again.

Chuck was the funniest guy I had ever worked for. He was about five-nine, a couple inches shorter than Gale, a little pudgy, and slightly balding. His sense of humor was an acquired taste, one might say. He was the type of man you either loved or hated. Most everyone loved him. His language was also quite colorful, and I have to admit, he may have been a bit prejudiced—not necessarily against people of color, but against ugly people. He made them the butt of all his jokes.

Chuck was also something of a prankster. He and I would play tricks on each other at any cost. Here are a few examples: Unbeknownst to me, he put shoe polish on my telephone receiver. He kept calling my extension and would whisper, "Pick up, pick up," making me think he had a secret to share. Every time I put the phone to my ear, I would get shoe polish on myself. Finally the smell gave it away, and I saw what he had done. Another time he found an old, dirty condom in the parking lot. He stuck it on my car antenna like a little flag. He loved to lick gummy bears and stick them to my eyeglass lenses, and I was always finding miscellaneous items in the bottom of my coffee cup. The dope could have choked me. He was forever sticking his finger in whatever food item was sitting on my desk. I think his favorite prank was to leave me phone messages. It would have a phone number and say to call whatever name he came up with. I would call the number and get an escort service for lonely women, a sign-up sheet for women looking for Russian husbands, or a gay-rights parade rally. Nothing was off-limits. In return, I mailed him back that used condom. It arrived the same day he had company from out of town; they were all standing together when he opened the envelope. Another time I found a dead moth in the office. Chuck's wallet was kept openly on his desk. I casually put the moth in his wallet and never gave it another thought. It so happened this particular day, he took several clients to lunch, and it was his turn to pay. When he opened his wallet, the dead moth fell out. You could hear the roar all over the restaurant, along with the question of "When was the last time you opened your wallet, Chuck?" Another time, I put a For Sale sign in the back window of his new truck asking for the "best offer" and gave his home phone number. It took him a while to get over the time I crumbled a few oatmeal-raisin cookies in the men's toilet. He started yelling at all the men in the office and accused them all of being pigs and not knowing how to flush. Chuck had a very weak stomach. Those cookies really do look nasty when they've been floating for a while.

Needless to say, Gale was never involved in any pranks. She was all business all the time. She actually accused me of trying to break up her marriage. The knucklehead just couldn't believe that her husband and I could just be friends. He told her I was like a sister to him. I don't know if she ever felt comfort from those words, and I don't think she ever really trusted me.

Gale did try to be a good friend to me. When I became ill, she thought nothing of driving about twenty miles from her house to mine to take me to the hospital. She offered to travel with me to Wisconsin when I had to go there for a special procedure. And she never hesitated to slip me a few hundred dollars for medical assistance when I came up short. I think it was just the idea of Chuck and me that bothered her. It's too bad I wasn't a little bit uglier; there would have never been any problems. Chuck would have totally ignored me except to make fun of me behind my back. Poor Gale—her load was heavy.

Another interesting character at Chuck's company was Bill. He was a six-foot Alaskan with the most inviting hazel eyes. He was responsible for me learning what the term "pencil dick" referred to. What a sweet guy. He loved having sex but was not well enough equipped for me to enjoy it. One day I had to address the embarrassing question to him, "Are you in yet?" I had to wiggle around to find out for myself. He was another frustrating man who touched my heart. I was sure I was never meant to have a really good sex life. Somebody once asked me if I was a lesbian. I answered, "Not yet." It was beginning to look like a definite choice to consider. Bill and I used to go upstairs to the conference room to fool around. I showed him a little trick I had learned involving ice cubes. That was not a good choice on my part. I had forgotten about cold making "things" smaller.

One Christmas, Gale sent Bill and me to Walmart to buy some office decorations. We decided to have a little pick-me-up in his van before we went in. When we returned a couple of hours later, Gale asked what took us so long. I believed Bill told her that the store had been closed, and he couldn't get in. What a punk!

After a couple of years, Chuck fired Bill. I always wondered if there wasn't maybe a bit of Dick mentality in that firing. Even though Chuck and I were never romantically involved, I think it bothered him somewhat to see me with Bill. Well, it was fun while it lasted.

We had the best Christmas parties. Chuck was very generous to his employees and always took us to really nice restaurants for either lunch or dinner. One year we had a Santa who handed us gifts that were designed especially for each of us. Birthdays were always celebrated as well, and summers were never without our share of backyard cookouts.

Life was not just fun and sex at this company. We worked very hard, and it was a very successful firm. Chuck would become quite wealthy when he sold the business several years later. He and Gale would live the life of luxury, although I would no longer be a part of it.

CHAPTER 21
A TRAGIC EVENT

Dick and I were drifting apart. Ginny was my whole life. She needed all my attention. Aside from a passionate night here and there, I was all hers. When Ginny was twelve, Dick died of cancer. When I heard he was in the hospital for the final time, the blood drained from my face, but I took her to see him. I will never get that sight out of my mind. This was the love of my life, the father of my child, and I hardly recognized him. He was a skeleton of a man with a gaunt face and sparse, white hair. My heart was breaking. All my memories of our time together came flooding back. I had to hold tight to them; I felt if I let go, I would lose them forever.

I looked over to Ginny, who said, "Okay, we can go now." She seemed to have no feelings for this man whatsoever. But why would she? He never was a part of her life.

Dick's funeral was private. Only immediate family members were invited. Although Ginny was a blood relative, she was not an official family member and therefore not invited. There was no way she would stand for that. I cried all day, so Margie drove us to the cemetery, where she and Ginny crashed the services. I waited in the car out of respect for his real wife. Margie and Ginny sat in the very back of the church, so as to not draw attention to themselves. That drew all kinds of attention. After the service, when people started walking back to them, they made a speedy exit. The two of them came running out of the church, where I was waiting for them in the getaway car.

Margie yelled, "Hit it!" They jumped in, and I laid rubber. I had never driven so fast in my life. My heart was beating as fast as the wheels were spinning. Off we went, and we never looked back. I cried for a week straight. How could Dick be gone? First Theresa had died, and now Dick. I didn't want to go on. My heart was overflowing with sorrow. I continued only out of necessity for my daughter.

Ginny overheard a phone conversation I had with Gale: "I can hardly look at Ginny without crying, because she reminds me so much of Dick." She took this to mean that I didn't want her around anymore. I can't believe some of the stupid things I say. I tried to assure her: "That is the farthest thing from my mind. I love you with my whole heart and soul, and I am ever so grateful you remind me of your father." It was a torturous year. On many a day, I was close to despair.

During this period of Ginny's life, she found herself strangely insecure. She would cry, "Why am I so ugly? Why don't boys like me?"

I kept assuring her, "Your boobs will grow, and your teeth can be fixed." (Her teeth were a bit crooked.) "In a few years, when it really counts, you will be beautiful, I promise." She was only twelve years old at the time. My predictions for her would come true: she would be a beautiful teenager. She needed to stop listening to those little urchins who were constantly teasing her.

I, on the other hand, was lonely and depressed, and as fate would have it, Ginny did turn into a teenager. I didn't know which event would kill me first: the loss of my love or Ginny's teen years. Something had to be done. Everything in Denver reminded me of places I had visited or things I had done with Dick. Ginny seemed to be mad at the world. After his death, I swear he came every night and sat on the edge of my bed. I never saw or heard him, but his presence was unmistakable. This would last for many years to come.

CHAPTER 22
BACK TO CALIFORNIA

IN 1995, AFTER WORKING FOR Chuck and Gale for almost eight years, Ginny and I moved back to Northern California. She was almost fourteen years old, and she told me that if we didn't move, she was sure she would end up on drugs and on the street. That was a good enough reason for me. As soon as her braces were removed, we packed our possessions and off we went, back to sunny California. My sister Margie came with us to help with the driving. Now, even though the move was Ginny's idea, like any normal teenager, the little wretch sulked all 1,300 miles. Our cat, Sadie Kathleen, shed about five pounds of hair during the trip. I kept that car for several years, and I never did get all the hair out of the upholstery. Nor could I get out the piece of chocolate Margie sat on. It became part of the driver's seat and always looked like I had had an accident every time someone noticed it. I could never convince them of hard it was to get chocolate out. That was before the days of OxiClean.

A few months after we arrived in California, I went back to work for Bill and Gina, the people I had worked for ten years earlier. Ginny started high school. She was beginning to get out of her funk, and I was learning to laugh again. This really was a fun company to work for. Everyone got along so well. Gina was about the total opposite of Gale. Did I mention that Bill and Gina were also married? Of course, they had been married even before they took over the company from Bill's father, so that could have made a difference, but I'm thinking it was more of a total personality difference.

I was strictly inside sales this time around and happy to be so. I loved having the phone as my security blanket.

Most people don't think of me as shy, but I really am. I have been self-conscious about my looks my whole life, and now I had a daughter who people said looked just like me. I didn't see how that could be. I thought Ginny was beautiful, and I was about the total opposite. Of course, she had her dad's genes as well—maybe that helped. Nope, that couldn't be. Dick hadn't been that good-looking, either. So that must mean that two not-so-good-looking people create a good-looking child. Yes, I'll go with that theory.

My daughter and I loved Northern California, especially San Francisco. We had been there several times before when we were still living in Denver. It was always our three-day-weekend getaway. We stayed in the big fancy hotels on Nob Hill and always had afternoon tea. Now that we lived in California, I could no longer afford the fancy hotels. Ginny, being a sweet emerging adult, always wanted to get back home the same day anyway—and the quickest route. She actually learned her way around the city better than I did. I was always lost. It was definitely the days before my GPS. Once Ginny got her driver's license, I was no longer needed for her weekly trips to the city. I seldom went alone, because as I said, I always got lost.

She may have known her way around many cities, but a great driver she was not. Ginny would total three cars before she turned twenty. Our insurance adjuster, Steve, would become a close friend to each of us.

Ginny did not have a storybook high-school experience. She was so bored all the time. I knew it was because she was too smart to be attending public school, but she didn't want to stand out by taking special classes. Meanwhile she became part of a crowd referred to as the "field savages." There was cheerleading, debate club, and drama club, just to mention a few activities she could have chosen, but my daughter chose to become a savage. I was so proud. She wore blue jeans, extra-large flannel shirts, and black stoner boots. This was her entire wardrobe throughout high school. It saved me money on school clothes—and, for that matter, school supplies. It seemed she skipped school every bit as often as she attended. At any given time, she only had one girlfriend; all the rest of her crowd was made up of knucklehead boys who filled her head with useless nonsense. Four or five of the boys might as well have been my own sons. They became known to Ginny and me simply as "the boys."

Mine was the hangout house, the cool place to be—probably because I lived across the street from the school, and I was at work all day. I prefer to believe it was because I was a cool mom. At least I always knew where my kid was, or so I let myself believe. When a shirt or jacket was left behind, I let them think they were lost forever. To this day, I still have someone's sweatshirt that brings me warmth on a cool Colorado evening.

I don't know where these boys shopped, but I sure did like their tastes.

One night Ginny was out with the boys. I took advantage of the quiet, peaceful night by indulging in a hot, relaxing bubble bath. While lying there, enjoying the solitude, I heard a humming noise coming from the other side of the wall—from Ginny's bedroom. When I went to investigate, I found that the walk-in closet had been turned into a little pot farm. New lighting had been hung and was giving life to five giant marijuana plants. Oh, my God! Was she kidding? Upon her return home that evening, she was confronted by a crazy mother. I questioned the new addition to our apartment.

"What were you thinking? Did you really think I wouldn't find this stuff? Do you realize it's against the law to grow pot?" She innocently answered that she was just doing a friend a favor (not one of the "boys"). The young man told her that his parents would not allow this venture in their home. Really, and they thought it would be okay in my home? I told her, "I want this stuff out of here by the time I get home from work tomorrow, and I want everything put back where it was."

She said "okay" and went on to bed. Nothing ever seemed to shake her. She never saw the harm or felony of her actions. For someone so smart, I thought she was awfully dumb.

Ginny may have pulled some crazy stunts, but she never forgot the lessons her grandpa had taught her about money. In those days, a person had to be sixteen to be able to buy cigarettes (she was only fifteen). She got one of the boys to buy her a pack of smokes and would then sell them to her customers for $.25 each. It took me a couple of weeks to confront her as to why so many kids were stopping by the house every morning before school. She told me what she was up to and how proud she was of herself for thinking up the way for making a few extra bucks. One thing about my daughter: she would tell me anything I asked her, but she would never just volunteer the information. So if I didn't feel I wanted to be aware of what was going on, I simply wouldn't ask. I really did thank God I only had one child. Her last school picture showed her wearing a T-shirt that read "Rehab is for quitters." No nice senior picture for me to display—no, sir, not from Ginny.

When she bought her first car, one of the "boys" did the test drive and assured me the car was in fine shape. It turned out the car barely had a working transmission. There was a few thousand dollars I would never see again. I still can't imagine what made me put such faith in a sixteen-year-old boy. To this day, she is still in touch with at least two of the boys. They are very successful and can laugh at the hoopla of their youths.

Ginny moved out to her own apartment when she was eighteen. She was working part time and going to college part time. The day she told me of her plans, I experienced my first migraine. Not ever having one before, I wasn't really sure what was happening. I thought for sure I was dying. My heart and my head had never experienced such torment.

Every week or so, Ginny would bring a plastic bag over to my apartment and do her grocery shopping. She was doing well on her own.

About a month before she turned nineteen, Ginny decided she wanted to move to, I believe, New York. She set out on a road trip all by herself from California to Oregon (my second migraine) to visit a friend of hers. All went well until she decided to surprise her grandparents in Denver. She got as far as Wyoming. Her car went over a cliff, tumbling bumper over bumper about three times before landing at the bottom. She, luckily, was not wearing a seat belt and got tossed out the driver's-side window halfway down the cliff.

Landing in a giant anthill, she appeared, to the naked eye, to have no physical injuries. There was no blood, although she was unconscious. Several people saw the accident, so help was only minutes away. A quick-thinking nurse noticed a small bump on the side of her head. Since they were just a small trauma center, they had her flown to Denver, the nearest major hospital equipped to handle severe head trauma. It turned out she had a blood clot on her brain, and they operated immediately.

My contact information was found, and I was notified just before she left for Denver. "Please don't be too alarmed," the nurse said. "She's unconscious, but the doctors in Denver will take good care of her." With the help of several of my co-workers, I caught the first plane to Denver to be with my daughter.

When I arrived, Ginny had just gotten out of surgery. I was told by the surgeon that she would need around-the-clock care, if she even lived through the night. She would need to learn everything again, from walking to talking to tending to her own needs. I experienced my third migraine. I called Gina, my boss, and gave her the grim prognosis. I tried to figure out how I would move back to Denver to care for my broken child.

As it turned out, she made it through the night, and one week later, she walked out of the hospital. The only evidence of her near-death experience was a shaven head and a big scar. Ginny was even beautiful bald. I stayed with her an extra few days after she was released from the hospital. She stayed with my sister Margie for another week or so.

Instead of going on to New York, Ginny decided to move back to California. Margie and I salvaged as many of her belongings from her smashed-up car as we could. I had them boxed up, and my mom had them shipped back to California. Ginny returned to me via the railroad. I was afraid to let her fly for fear her little head would explode when the plane gained altitude. None of the medical professionals could believe Ginny's recovery. They had written her off as dead or at least severely damaged. My miracle child had been given a second chance; she was the talk of the hospital.

A few weeks later, Ginny turned nineteen, and her medical insurance expired. It's all in the timing.

I had turned fifty the year before, and people kept reminding me that it was time to get married. How had fifty gotten there so fast? I still wasn't ready. I couldn't worry about Ginny and a man. It was around this time that I became an *X-Files* freak. My entire office was cluttered with memorabilia from the TV show and every article I could find about the stars. I had *X-Files* souvenirs from clothing to pictures to knickknacks of all sorts, even the action figures. I had heard there was going to be a Scully marathon in San Francisco one particular weekend. I had to attend. I showed up at the hotel, paid my entrance fee, and proceeded inside. I was so excited I could hardly contain myself. I didn't even get lost looking for the hotel in the downtown area. As everyone began arriving, I noticed everyone was female. It seemed this was the lesbian charter fan club for Scully. *Oh, my God!* I even got hit on once. Nervously, I left before the show got started and the lights went down. I did win a door prize, though, so the trip wasn't a total bust. Another time, I flew to Los Angeles for the day when I heard Gillian Anderson was going to be in a Christmas show of some sort. I was only an hour's flight away, so again, I figured I just had to go. I took a taxi from the airport to the theater. This time there were both men and women. I was beginning to feel better, but then I realized they were all gay. What the heck? Were all Scully's followers gay? Apparently a good deal of them were. But I met Ellen DeGeneres and actually got to speak to Gillian Anderson. She not only gave me her autograph, but she also had her driver call me a cab so I could get back to the airport. What a fun day.

The next time I saw Gillian Anderson was at an AIDS run in San Francisco. I climbed over the fence, since I had no intention of running any race. I just wanted to see her talk. A guard let me right up front by the stage; because I'm sure he thought I was some sort of nutty lady who was perfectly harmless. He never took his eye off me, though. After her little talk, she was swooped away in a golf cart; I guess she had no intention of running, either.

I never did meet the actor who played Mulder, David Duchovny, but I did meet the Cigarette-Smoking Man. He was the star attraction at an electronic show our industry held every year in California. I was privileged to work his booth. I took pictures of him with all his fans. I even have a few of my own. What a glorious couple of days. Everyone said our isle was "where it was happening." I do tend to get a bit carried away when I become obsessed with a new passion. But like any true fan, I disappeared along with the show when it went off the air. My new passion, once again, was the Old West.

Meanwhile my health was not getting any better. I left Colorado with a troubled pancreas. The doctors there knew the problem was pancreas divisum but did not know how to resolve the issue. It was not life threatening but quite painful. I was told surgery was my only option. The trick was to find a surgeon who could do the deed.

My boss, Gina, had a good friend who was a nurse at Stanford Hospital. She got me hooked up with a big-shot doctor who felt he was up to the challenge of removing part of, and rerouting, my pancreas. The procedure is called a whipple. It is rare and extremely difficult to perform, with only a 30 percent chance of success. I was not among the lucky 30 percent. I still have chronic pancreatitis and am told I will be cursed with this ailment the rest of my life. Narcotics were my only friends. A nerve block to something around the pancreas would be a solution, but I'm told they only perform those on patients who have less than a year to live. I know how crazy that sounds, but that is part of my life. I walked around with a drainage tube coming out of my tummy for six weeks after the surgery. It kept getting clogged with things like scrambled eggs and noodles—things I wasn't supposed to eat for this very reason. My poor Ginny had to assist every time I needed to get declogged; in another year, she would enter nursing school. It took about nine months, but I finally made a full recovery from the whipple.

A year and a half later, on Ginny's twenty-first birthday, I was diagnosed with breast cancer. A woman who I absolutely could not stand is credited with my finding the tumor. Her husband was a regular customer of ours. One day he came in and said his wife had been given the dreaded news of breast cancer. All the ladies in the office immediately went home that night and did a self—exam. Bingo: I had a lump. I was in the process of sending Ginny off to another college, this time in Delaware. I did not want anything to interrupt this trip or influence her decision to go. I decided to wait until I got back home to see a doctor. That date just happened to be her twenty-first birthday.

I was told I had stage two breast cancer and needed speedy surgery. Well, the first thing I thought of was my promise to my old friend Theresa: if I were ever diagnosed with cancer, I would not let them operate. I informed the doctor of my decision. As you can imagine, this did not sit well with any of them. I was told medicine had progressed a great deal in the past twenty years, and if Theresa had been given the same prognosis today, she would probably still be alive. They eventually wore me down, and off I went to surgery.

The doctor said she got the tumor and several infected lymph nodes as well. I was scheduled for six to eight rounds of chemotherapy. I quit after two rounds. All my hair fell out, and I was so weak I wanted to die. Of course I didn't. My daughter went along with my decision to quit chemo, believing I knew what was best for my body. This was in March of 2003. I was told I wouldn't live out the year. Well, I am obviously still here, so I guess doctors don't know everything. My hair grew back as a white afro. Now there's a conversation starter. Ginny left Delaware and came home. It was about this time she entered nursing school. She was determined to take care of her poor old mama. God, I loved that young lady.

A few months after my two rounds of chemo had ended and my white afro had started to grow in, I decided I wanted to go on a wagon train ride. I felt I deserved a little vacation, but I didn't necessarily want to go alone. My friends from work all had to work, and not a one showed the least bit of interest in accompanying me on my venture. So good ol' sister Charlotte volunteered . . . sort of. I gave her a list of items she would need for the trip, and we met up in Jackson Hole, Wyoming. It would be a three-day, two-night adventure in a covered wagon traveling through the Grand Tetons. What a kick. Of course all the young cowboys swooned over Charlotte as if she were some sort of prize catch. I don't think they even cared that she was two and three times their age. She looked good in her cowgirl attire, and that's all that seemed to matter. I had even dyed my hair, and nobody swooned over me. It was high school all over again. But at least my dream of being on a wagon train had finally been obtained.

The following year, Charlotte and Precious took me to Salem, Massachusetts—another dream of mine from when I was into the occult a very long time ago. I have to admit I was a little uneasy while roaming the town. I was sure a witch would appear from under a tree or something. I kept a close hold on Charlotte and a close eye on Precious. Nobody was going to ditch me in this town. I still have a souvenir branch I brought back from a witch's hanging tree. Pretty cool, huh?

I had only one close-call clandestine relationship while working for Bill and Gina. Terry and I were sent on a business trip together to, of all places, Denver. We stayed at a curious hotel that resembled a castle. He proceeded to get me drunk the first night we were there. He wanted to invite me to his room but ended up puking all over his bed instead. We did go shopping the next day and remained good friends for many years after. I was not interested in romance at that time. I was still mourning Dick, even though several years had passed. Simply talking about him still brought me to tears.

CHAPTER 23
MOVING ON . . . BACK TO COLORADO

IN 2005 I MOVED BACK to Denver. My parents were getting old, and I felt they needed me to be a little closer than California. The year before, my old friend and teacher, Kit, had died from a heart attack. It made me realize how precious life really was. I had had a dream about Kit one night—one of those dreams that seemed so real I felt as if I were really with her. The next day, I called my mother to say I was coming to Denver for a few days' vacation. When I arrived, I told her of my plans to visit Kit. She immediately showed me a newspaper clipping she had saved for me. Kit had died the very night of my dream. Creepy, huh?

I left Ginny in California to finish nursing school. Leaving her was like leaving a part of my soul. I told myself I had to live each day as it came and not dwell on regrets nor worries about the future; both the past and the future were beyond my power to influence. I went back to work for the first distributor I had worked for almost twenty years earlier, where I had met Gerald and Pauline. They had both moved on but still stayed in touch.

Speaking of keeping in touch, Manny was calling on a more regular basis again. He had retired from the service but still kept busy with his top-secret jobs. He knew better than to tell me too much, but it was always so good to hear from him. I think I finally fell out of love with him, but he will always remain my number-one best friend.

Ginny finished her schooling. She was now a nurse but tired of living in California. She packed her car and Sadie the cat and headed for, of all places, Seattle. She knew exactly two people in the entire city. Little facts like that never seemed to bother her. She held down two nursing jobs while getting to know her way around the city. At this time, her best friend from high school was getting married in Hawaii. Ginny was to be a bridesmaid. Off she went to Hawaii, where she met, of all people, Manny. He just happened to be there on some sort of business. During one of our yearly conversations, Manny and I had realized he and Ginny would be only a few miles from each other during that weekend. I gave him her phone number, and they arranged a meeting. They got together one evening and talked for hours. She told him she had heard about him all her life and was most anxious to see what all the fuss was about. They had a great visit, but she never understood the connection we had. She did find out he held the same affection for me as I did for him, minus the puppy love. I was just his good ol' buddy, Betty.

At this wedding, Ginny met the groom's cousin, Nick. She and Nick formed an instant friendship. As it turned out, they lived only a few miles apart back in Washington. Long story short, to this day they are living together in the wilderness of Monroe, Washington.

Ginny's cat, Sadie, died after sixteen years of being a constant and loving companion. She went into a sad state of depression that lasted a couple of months. Thank God Nick was around to be a sturdy shoulder for her grief. She never got another cat. Her choice of animals returned to dogs—really big dogs. To this day, the death of Sadie remains a tearful remembrance.

I believe my parents were glad I had moved back. I found an apartment a few miles from their new townhouse. They had sold their old house a few years back for something smaller and easier to maintain. It was—is—a beautiful house, with windows everywhere. I really like all that natural light. It was in a brand-new community a few miles from the airport. This made it easier when my sister Charlotte came to Denver or Margie left. My parents were their unofficial chauffeurs. At this time, my sisters were both still working for the airlines, and a ten-minute trip to the airport was much easier than the thirty minutes they used to have to endure.

Ginny's second cat, Cleo, made the move with me back to Colorado. Cleo had been adopted from the Humane Society in California shortly after she returned from Delaware. The trip back to Denver was not the hairy mess I had experienced ten years earlier. My sister Charlotte and her husband, "Precious," helped me with the drive back to Denver. He had told Charlotte at one time that he was allergic to cats, but she didn't believe him. Just in case he was on the level, we decided not to tell him about Cleo until the day we packed the car and headed out. As it turned out, he really was allergic to cats. About an hour into our journey, his eyes started watering and swelled to almost twice their size. We made a quick stop for some antihistamine and went on our merry way, never to doubt his word again. Cleo sure loved him; she insisted on staying as close to him as possible. The man was amazingly patient with all three of us women.

Other than the allergic reaction, a small snowstorm in Salt Lake City, a rainstorm in western Colorado, and Cleo getting stuck under a bed in one of the hotels, the trip was pretty uneventful.

While working for the current distributor, I met Billy. He was a young man thirteen years my junior. We became quite close and bummed around together despite our age difference. We took a little vacation together to Wyoming. I wanted to go to Cody, and he wanted to see Yellowstone. We took my SUV, in which he did most of the driving. Our first stop was Cody, Wyoming. I loved all the shopping and being with someone who also enjoyed it. We spent one night there, and then off we went.

On our way to Yellowstone, I explained to him why I was so uncomfortable in the woods. It brought back terrible memories of my nineteenth birthday. The situation was awkward, to say the least. It seemed to go in one ear and out the other. He took his sweet time driving through those trees and forests. The terror I had once felt would obviously never fade from my memory. We finally made it out of the wilderness and headed for home. We went by way of Jackson Hole, one of my favorite places. I think the foolish man felt he would win my favor back if we could get back to civilization and shopping. He was correct, but it only lasted a short time; after arriving back home, I remembered how furious I was at him for not taking my feelings more seriously. Our friendship was never the same after that trip. Billy would soon become just another man who had disappointed me.

I got laid off about two and a half years into my employment. I was happy to go, since I had been secretly looking for a new job anyway. The fact that they made the first move got me six or eight weeks' severance pay. It only took me two weeks to find a new place to call home, so moneywise, I made out just fine. This new job would be my last. I had less than four years to go to be entitled to social security, and I was counting down each miserable year. The closer I came to retirement, the less patience I had for working. Nothing at that job pleased me except for a few new friends I had made. Billy remains a fond memory.

CHAPTER 24
The End Is Near

MY NEW AND LAST JOB was for another distributor that was nothing like the previous employer; this was a privately owned company. The owner was a delightful old gentleman named Hanspeter, from Germany. My immediate boss was Raphael, from Switzerland, and just because his accent sounded German, it was not a good idea to call him a German. I started out in inside sales, my usual fallback position. That's what they were looking for, and it seemed to pay the most, so I was their gal.

My boss, RB, as I came to call him, was a most unique individual. On a good day, he could be a most delightful and empathetic person. If you catch him on an off day, which I had no problem doing, the tears would flow with no shame whatsoever. I had never had a job where I openly cried so much, and RB did not like it at all. I guess he thought telling me to stop crying should be all it took. Well, maybe in his world. Mine is a very emotional world, and always has been. I did not like being in the sales department. The people were nice enough, but the stress was taking its toll on me. The salespeople answering the phones were a big deal in this company. I loved answering them, but when I did, I was accused of hogging the business. When I didn't answer the calls, I was accused of being lazy—a no-win situation for sure. RB just wanted everybody to do everything and not complain. Fat chance. He worked with five saleswomen and one man.

Around this time, my Uncle Junior died of cancer. What a horrific time. He was the unofficial head of the family, and everyone looked to him for advice, support, and of course, a good time. I personally was overcome with a heavy heart. Life would never be the same again, not without Uncle Junior. My Aunt Joyce was especially close to him, being his younger sister. One day in the hospital, while waiting for him to die, Aunt Joyce let out this howl of sorrow and compared herself to a wet noodle. As sad as I was, I had to laugh. Of course, I excused myself from the family before letting go. Where do people get these expressions? There was no funeral or hoopla of any kind; Uncle Junior wanted it that way, and the family granted his final wishes. We all kept a tiny bit of his ashes, or at least his sisters and I did. I still miss Uncle Junior. In my imagination, I often revisit those carefree days of our European trip. Sadly, less than a year later, my own dear dad died, also of cancer. What a dreadful disease. My poor mom was losing all the men in her life.

Six months after my dad died, Mom fell in her backyard and broke her hip. As she was lying in the backyard for hours, under the sprinkler, Mom kept yelling for help: "Help me, please! Someone help!" A passerby finally heard her cries and summoned help. After surgery and a few weeks of physical therapy, she went back home. She recovered but has never really been the same. My sisters and I were very concerned about her living there alone in the townhouse. She had no close friends and no neighbors she could count on.

After experiencing life in the rehab center, she was open to exploring the possibility of moving into a retirement village. We were confident she would make friends and be much happier there than living alone, several miles from me or my sister Margie. Charlotte lived in Reno. So there we were, off on the hunt for the perfect residence. It really wasn't hard to find one, and in a couple of months, she made the permanent move. She was going to put the townhouse up for sale, but the market was so bad, she would have had to take a huge hit if she went that route. I was asked to move into the house until the market turned around—about a year. Yeah, that didn't happen. Almost two years later, I'm still in the house. No regrets, though—I love this house and all its windows. My friend Diana helped me move all my stuff and some of hers into my new home. She was a cowgirl from Montana and had a lot of Western decor she no longer used. Oh, my God, I was in heaven. I transformed my mom's empty house into a Western wonderland. Now I really love it here. My family couldn't even believe it was the same house.

After I had been with the company a little over a year, I began smelling smoke. There was no rhyme or reason for the smell. It would hit me any time of the day and any day of the week. I searched Google for my symptoms. It seemed I either had a sinus infection or a brain tumor. I immediately e-mailed my doctor—DB, as she came to be known—and informed her of my manifestations.

"Do you mind if I do some blood work before we take a drastic step and scan your head?" she asked.

An exam was done as well as blood tests. We finally did the CAT scan. She just didn't want to believe I had a brain tumor, but the symptoms persisted. I was also getting several headaches on a daily basis. I thought perhaps they were the result of the amount of narcotics I was ingesting. Collectively, we decided to try to get me clean. A few different drugs were tried to replace the narcotics for the pain of my pancreatitis. Nothing was working, and I was being subjected to all sorts of side effects. Half of the time, I wasn't sure where I was, or I would get lost driving home from work. I would buy things and not remember, later just finding new purchases in my closet. I was so confused at work and appeared to be drugged most of the time. It was at this time I was also experiencing unassisted orgasms at work and at home. All these symptoms seemed to be the result of trying too many different drugs in a short period of time.

During this time, I met my spirit lady, as I called her. This spirit lady poked me on the arm and motioned with her finger to follow her. I was so freaked, I just sat there. When I jumped up to follow her, she had turned the corner and disappeared. I took this to mean she wanted me to follow her into another world. That was the first serious thought I had of ending my life.

I told DB about the spirit lady.

"DB, I think I'm in trouble."

"What kind of trouble?" she asked.

I told her about the spirit lady and her intentions of taking me away. DB contacted a shrink friend of hers for advice. He suggested I contact the behavior unit at Kaiser and do some serious talking to a professional—someone other than DB. That was when I first met Jamie, a social worker. She didn't feel I was crazy or neurotic and, after hearing my story, just let me go on my merry way. Apparently it's okay, with her, to see spirits as long as they don't talk to you.

The other symptoms grew worse. DB decided it was time to look a little further and have an MRI scheduled. The MRI showed a small tumor, but the doctors didn't seem to be too concerned about it and didn't feel it was causing the smoke smell or the other symptoms. DB, also, was more concerned about the crazy effects the new drugs were having on me than the tiny tumor. We decided to put me back on oxycodone, my drug of choice, which seemed to cause the least amount of crazy in me.

I finally talked RB into letting me out of sales and into the order-entry department. There I met my two new best friends, Kathleen and Kristen, the crackhead. Now, everybody liked Kathleen, who was kind, smart, and very religious—unlike the crackhead, who was only smart. She had a few followers in the warehouse group, but the salespeople referred to her as El Diablo. I liked the punk and got on very well with her. She said it was because our personalities were so similar. Both of us were grouchy and got irritated quite easily. I had to remind her that I was twenty-five years her senior, and I had more of a right to be a hag than she did, especially at her tender age of thirty-five. She didn't care; she was mean and cantankerous, and that was how one had to accept her. Love her or leave her—that was her outlook. I grew to love her as sort of an adopted daughter. We went shopping almost every weekend; she drove, and I bought lunch. When we weren't shopping, she was constantly nagging me to call Billy for some much-needed romance. I had given up on romance ages ago.

The other lady in the office was Joyce, the mean lady. For some reason, she also got along with the crackhead Kristen, but her personality was more like Kathleen's—except if you irritated her. Then she got really mean.

These three ladies were lifesavers to me in the last six months of my employment.

A few months after settling in my new department, I was diagnosed with epilepsy. One more thing, right? I never believed I had the ailment. Neither did DB, my primary doctor, but the neurosurgeon who read my MRI said the smelling of smoke was a sign of seizures. He asked this little tiny doctor, Dr. H., with a long blond ponytail, to write me a prescription for anti-seizure medication. This really set things in motion. If I had been acting crazy before, now I was ready for the loony bin. I was having seizure like symptoms, one after another. The poor ladies in my department had to cope with all the craziness. Over the summer, I was admitted to every hospital in the immediate area by way of several different ambulance companies. One of the paramedics even made a return trip and remembered me.

During my first hospital visit, the head nurse from the emergency room told me I could call upon her for anything I needed. It turned out I needed her at about four o'clock the next morning. In my drugged state, I wanted to call my friend Kathleen. My nurse refused to give me the phone at this early hour. I made such a fuss asking for the head nurse that they finally had to summon her. She gave me the phone, and the call was made to Kathleen, who was happy to take the call. I don't know why I was kept so drugged. All I wanted to eat was this fabulous cherry cobbler from their menu. I got more cherries on my gown than I did in my mouth, but I was determined to eat it every chance I had. I was not a very good patient and kept insisting that they let me out.

On the third day, when they decided they couldn't find the source of the seizures, they were only too happy to let me go. I had to assure them I wouldn't be home alone—a lie, but I assured them. I arrived home, minus my socks they stole, and continued in this state for another two days until all the drugs finally wore off. This trip to the hospital made Dr. H. quite nervous; she couldn't figure out what was going on, so she increased the anti-seizure meds and told me I couldn't drive for three months. My good friends from work would take on the chore of driving me to and from work as well as other places I needed to go.

My second hospital trip was a catastrophe. This time my underwear was stolen, and when I eventually went home, I had to go commando. They kept me just as drugged as the first hospital, but this time, I informed them that I was DNR (do not resuscitate). Well, this just made them get all crazy, and in come the shrinks. I was asked if I had a death wish. I assured them I did not, but if I died for some reason, I didn't want them to take it upon themselves to decide I needed to come back. If a person dies, he's meant to be dead. I didn't want to be turned into a zombie. There was no cherry cobbler here, so I was most anxious to go home.

Still the tiny neurologist was stumped. She assumed I was just stressed. If I was, she was the one stressing me. I still never believed I had epilepsy.

My third hospital was the only one left in the area. I don't remember the food at all. I just remember this is where they finally decided my seizures weren't caused by epilepsy. I'm not sure of the doctor's name, but turns out he was a really good friend of the tiny doctor who had first prescribed the anti-seizure meds. He assured me she would figure out what was going on. I guess she's still working on that. She did call me after I returned home and apologized for giving me meds that were making me even sicker. Gee, do you think? I was finally taken off all the anti-seizure medications. It took me days to sober up.

Nobody could figure out what was causing the seizures, but they finally listened to me and stopped the anti-seizure meds. Their unsatisfying conclusion seemed to be, "It could be the tumor, we doubt it . . . could be stress, we doubt it . . . could be we will never know what is causing them."

On Ginny's twenty-ninth birthday, my cat Cleo died. She had never been sick a day in all her seven years until the week before her death. So in spite of all my medical worries, I was devastated by Cleo's illness. I had been touched by yet another death in my life, and I was sick with despair. Crackhead Kristen stayed with me during my time of sorrow. Little Cleo died in my arms. My broken heart could not be consoled. I am an animal lover, and it took a couple months, but I eventually rescued two new kittens, Lily and Leroy. Joy was in my life, and I was happy once again. These two cats drew on my heartstrings the moment I laid eyes on them. You just know when it's the right pet. Now the two are inseparable. I can't imagine one without the other, and I can't imagine me without either one of them.

The last time I was in the hospital, due to a bad reaction to a spinal tap, the drugs took a rather nasty toll on me. I was put back on anti-seizure meds, even though my doctors had previously decided I couldn't tolerate them. I became angry and belligerent. I did not yield easily. I begged them to let me go home, so I could put an end to my existence. Well, it seemed they couldn't just do that. Someone, a nurse or doctor, informed my daughter, who was living in Monroe, of my condition. She was told that if she didn't come and get me, they were going to send me the nuthouse for a few days until I could calm down. It was Thanksgiving Day.

Ginny caught an evening flight to Denver and came to swoop me up. I have very little memory of that hospital stay except that I was constantly trying to get out of bed, and they were constantly trying to keep me in it. I was sure I was well enough to go home on my own, but every time they let me try to get up alone, I landed on the floor. For some reason, this really irritated the nurses. I was calling my friends and daughter at all hours, telling them of the mistreatment I had to endure. But they all appeared ignorant and useless. I told myself I didn't care if I ever saw any of them again. Nobody was ever so happy to see Ginny enter a room as the nurses and doctors in the hospital. They said all I had to do was take a few steps on my own and keep my head up, and I could be released. I looked like a total freak trying to do it, but I did it, and I was put in a wheelchair and happily escorted out of the hospital. Ginny was their new hero.

She took me and my two cats back to Monroe with her a day later. I was still so drugged; I barely remember any of that. The first three days at her house, I kept asking her what I was doing there. The drugs were taking forever to wear off. She told me the story over and over as to why I was at her house. I finally called Jamie, the social worker, to get the whole story. I was so shocked. A nuthouse? Really? I was sure I would not live through this.

My two weeks in Monroe were not just vacation days. Ginny had me help her with her dog-food business. She has a gourmet dog-food business in addition to her nursing job. I was making dog food until I felt it was coming out of my ears. I had been left with exact instructions on the proper way to get the perfect results. She was not really happy with my culinary skills. I was not really happy with the arrangement. She actually lives about an hour outside of Seattle on some acreage with Nick and, at the time, one really big dog. (She now has three really big dogs.)

One day I decided to get out of the house for some fresh air. I walked about half a block before I turned around and ran home. I was sure a wild dog had his hungry eye on me. I never left the house alone again. My daughter found this humorous, as she routinely walked her dog several miles in the area and had never had a problem with this crazy-eyed dog. Hmmmm. The wilderness life is not for me. I need a city, and I need stores, neither of which was available within a twenty-minute drive. I was actually looking forward to going back to Denver.

I had e-mailed DB and told her I was coming home. I asked her if she still wanted to be my doctor. I knew I had gone a little mad when I was in the hospital, and I wasn't sure she felt comfortable with me anymore.

Her response was a positive one: "I am happy to continue taking care of you." She wrote, "And I am looking forward to seeing you next week." Yeah, that didn't last long. I did see her a few times before things got hairy.

My cats and I went home, and life went on as usual. I was actually quite happy to leave the wilderness of Monroe, Washington. The seizures seemed to have stopped for a while, but the smoke smell was just as strong.

I got these strange lumps on my legs, I was sure I had the dreaded blood clots that would travel to my heart and kill me. No, DB said, older people just get lumpy, and that was my case. I was becoming a lumpy old lady at the age of sixty-one.

The seizures stopped, but the headaches and pancreatitis were persistent. I just kept trying to get by. My crackhead friend was always there for me. I could always count on her, on both workdays and weekends. She called on a regular basis to make sure I was still functioning. Kathleen was there for me, too, but I usually had to call her instead of vice versa. She may not have been physically around, but she and her family were constantly praying for me, especially her daughter, Beanie. Beanie would lay hands on my head and pray for the tumor to go away. She was sure the tumor was causing the seizures.

The doctors finally gave up on me. I became suicidal. All those times in my past when I had wished for death were nothing compared to this. If my medical conditions weren't going to kill me, I would do it myself. There was no one I could turn to for comfort. Theresa was gone; Dick was gone; and I felt Ginny would be better off without me. No one else seemed to really matter at that point. I had begun to depend on DB for everything—everything medical, that is. When she told me my conditions were becoming too complicated for her, and she wanted me to start seeing specialists instead of her, I totally lost it. How could she just throw me aside after three years? How could I not matter to her anymore? Just like that, she could decide to stop taking care of me?

I knew I only had a couple more months until I retired. I was so scared that if DB could just toss me aside, the whole world might do the same. Going on was unthinkable. Fear persisted. Good God, perhaps I really was mad. Life became unthinkable. I decided to drop my cats off at the vet to be declawed and head for the nearest hospital.

It had snowed the previous day, so there was snow piled everywhere in the parking lot. I parked as close as possible, so I could go in and get it over with. I was going to take a bunch of pills there in the waiting room. I figured this way; nobody would have to find my rotting body in my car. They would find me in the hospital and cart my devastated and bloated body down to the morgue, and everyone's life would go on without me.

The lobby was warm and inviting against the cold, wintery weather outside. It was about seven in the evening, so I didn't see many people: a few security guards, one customer at the coffee cart, and a few others scattered about. I bought a cup of coffee and sat down away from the others. When it came time to take the first pill, I reached in my purse. Instead of pulling out the pills, I pulled out the card for a suicide hotline that Jamie had given me several months earlier.

This lady answered the phone. "Kaiser Help Center. How can I help you?"

"I wish I were dead, and I think I'm about to take a bunch of pills," I replied.

"Where are you? Are you somewhere safe?"

"I'm in a hospital in Parker."

She was so clever; I really have to give her credit. She got me to tell her my exact location in the hospital without ever actually asking me: "Are you warm enough? Are you by the door? Are there people around you? Are you wearing a coat?"

When she asked me what kind of purse I had, I started to become suspicious. Why in the world would a suicide-prevention lady care what kind of purse I was carrying? Was she caring more about fashion than the life hanging on by a thread? Just as I started to question her, I looked up, and there stood a nurse and two security guards. Oops, busted! The nurse suggested that I come with her and talk for a few minutes. By the size of the two guards, I didn't really think it was a suggestion. I accompanied them.

The nurses were also very clever. They said they just wanted to take my blood pressure to make sure I was okay. They asked if I had been drinking. I said no, but they proceeded to administer a Breathalyzer, which of course read zero. Before I knew it, I was talked out of my clothes and into a hospital gown. I kept insisting I couldn't stay at their hospital, because my insurance was not honored there. No problem, I was told—they had already cleared it with the insurance company. Were they kidding? I had only been there fifteen minutes. How could they get all that done in such a short time? Well, they had, and once again I was a prisoner in a hospital—although this time, I was sure to mind my p's and q's. I was there to die, not to be sent to the loony bin.

I sat there all night, drinking coffee and getting to know the three different guards I had posted outside my door, all taking shifts. The room was empty except for the bed and a big armchair. There was nothing I could possibly hurt myself with. All they would allow me was my phone; I told them I would have to call my boss if I were going to be late for work the next day. When it was time for one of my pain meds, they brought it to me.

I kept asking when I could go home but was told I had to wait until morning, when a shrink would come and talk to me. One of three things would happen, the guard told me: one, I could go home and forget all this had happened; two, I could be admitted for a seventy-two-hour hold; or three, I could be sent to the loony bin. This scared the hell out of me. The guard said not to worry. He said to just tell them how sorry I was and that I would never even think of trying to take my own life again—basically, tell them what they wanted to hear. Actually, I never did try to take my life; I just talked about it. I really didn't see the crime in that. Apparently, it is not a good conversation starter to say you wish you were dead. Who knew?

Anyway, I got through that, and they let me go home in the morning, as soon as I talked to the shrink. She didn't feel I was a danger to myself or to anyone else. I told her how sad I was about DB giving up on me, and for some reason, everyone then turned their attention to the bad DB. I was now the innocent bystander who had gotten smacked down by my doctor. I called my boss, RB, and told him I wouldn't be in because I had just been released from the hospital. He never asked why I was in the hospital. I guess he figured it was the same old seizure stuff. I had to go see three different shrinks over the next two weeks, just to make sure I was stable. I guess I passed as stable, because I was totally released by all the smooth-talking shrinks. I still kept in touch with Jamie, my very first smooth talker, just in case.

I continued to see DB, although things had become a little tense. I didn't feel comfortable talking to her, and I think she was always a little afraid I was still suicidal. Hmm . . . she couldn't get rid of me that easily. But the discomfort finally got the best of me, and I searched the bios of the other doctors at Kaiser to see if I could find one more suited to my needs. I did. She was said to be at ease caring for patients with multiple chronic conditions. She sounded like the gal for me. I wrote her an e-mail and asked if she felt she was up to the challenge of taking me on. If she agreed, I would be happy to join her practice. She took me on.

In a couple months, I think she started to regret her decision. I'm the chatty e-mailing sort, and she apparently is not fond of that sort. I'm trying to go easy on her. I don't want to be thrown out of Kaiser altogether by using up all their doctors. While keeping my headaches and pancreatitis under control, she discovered I have some sort of heart flutter. Surprise, surprise: another thing wrong with me!

Well, I gave up trying to put an end to my life. I figured if it ended by my own hand, my soul would be condemned to float in outer space, dodging space junk for all eternity. I was just going to have to wait for a natural ending.

That brings us up to date. I retired a few months ago. My mom still lives in the retirement village; Charlotte and Precious are still in Reno; Margie and her husband, Keith, still live here in Denver; and my love child, Ginny, is still in Monroe, Washington. My cats, Leroy and Lily, are healthy and happy and pretty much run my life. Retirement is everything I had hoped it would be, and even more. Manny is living in North Carolina. I hear from him at least a couple times a year. I lost touch with Dough Belly Jane several years ago. I'm not sure what happened to her. DB is still practicing, even without me. And the new doc hasn't kicked me to the curb—yet. Kathleen and the Crack-head are still close by. These were the main characters in my life. I couldn't have gone this far without them. Hopefully they will remain in my life for a few more chapters, although I do believe that DB has permanently left my life.

If all this nonsense hadn't happened with DB, I doubt I would be writing this book. She actually saved my life by telling me that no matter what happened between us, she would always be there for me. She would never abandon me, even though I feel I sort of abandoned her. She remains in my thoughts. I remember the little dance she did when she thought we had found a solution to my pain. I remember the sadness in her face when she told me of her sick little dog and having to put him down. I remember the nervous look she had when she told me her little boy wanted to ride the bus to school with the big kids. He was only going to be in kindergarten. I remember her asking me if I would miss her when she took a three-week vacation. I had never been away from her that long in the three years she had been my doctor. I had to admit that yes, I would miss her very much. I remember all the times she assured me I would be fine, even though I thought for sure I was dying. She had the most perfect skin I had ever seen on an adult. Her face was like a porcelain doll. Yes, thanks to DB, I finally wrote the book so many people over the years have told me I should write.

I was going to dedicate this book to DB, but upon my quest to get her permission, I decided against it. When I confronted her, she acted more as if I were asking for permission to poke her in the eye than to dedicate a book to her. People tried to make me aware of her lack of bedside manner, but I always just saw what I wanted to see. I didn't want to see the reaction she showed me, so once again, I got shot down and kicked in the gut, and I just plainly had to swallow yet another bitter pill. I still believe she is responsible for me writing this book, but that is as far as I care to take it.

If I am in a coma, I hope I never wake up. I would really hate to lose this life. Who knows what would be in store for a sixty-two-year-old coma victim with no job skills?